100 Best Recipes
for
100 Years
from
McCormick

100 Best Recipes
for
100 Years
from
McCormick

Recipe Development and Food Styling:
      Linda Armor and Lorraine Kealiher,
      McCormick Research Kitchens
Art Direction and Project Manager: Diane Hamel
Editor: John W. Felton
Art and Design: Tom Brecklin, Christine Coleman
Production Manager: Maura May

McCormick gratefully acknowledges the following for giving permission to McCormick &
Company, Inc., to include their trademarks in this book.

      Coca-Cola, "The Real Thing" – The Coca-Cola Company
      Noxzema – Noxell Corporation
      MICKEY MOUSE – The Walt Disney Company
      Monopoly – Parker Brothers
      Reebok® – Reebok International Ltd.
      Cabbage Patch™–Original Appalachian Artworks, Inc.

In addition, we extend special thanks to the American Spice Trade Association for the spice
illustrations on pages 36, 65, 88, 104, 109, 118, and 131.

Produced and published by The Benjamin Company, Inc.
                    One Westchester Plaza
                    Elmsford, NY 10523

Library of Congress Cataloging-in-Publication Data
100 best recipes for 100 years from McCormick.
      p.   cm.
   Bibliography: p.
   Includes index.
   ISBN 0-87502-234-0
   1. Cookery.   2. McCormick & Co. (Hunt Valley, Md.)–History.
3. United States–Social life and customs–History–19th century.
4. United States–Social life and customs–History–20th century.
I. McCormick & Co. (Hunt Valley, Md.) II. Title: One hundred best
recipes for one hundred years from McCormick.
TX714.A18   1988
641.5–do19   88-71046
                                                    CIP

*To the thousands of McCormick employees
who have been providing ''a whole world of good tastes''
for more than 100 years — and are now working on the next 100!*

Contents

Preface

This book celebrates over 100 years of "a whole world of good tastes" from McCormick & Company, Inc.

Today's billion-dollar firm, now recognized as the international leader in spices, seasonings and flavorings, began in a basement in downtown Baltimore, Maryland, when a man named Willoughby M. McCormick and three assistants started making fruit syrups on a warm September morning in 1889.

From the first, Willoughby's motto was "Make the Best—Someone Will Buy It." In that same spirit, we hope these "100 best recipes for 100 years from McCormick" provide you with a century of the best of tastes. We also hope they help to track the evolution and development of the Company through ten decades that brought dramatic changes in American lifestyles and eating habits.

The Beginning

Mark Twain called the late 1880s the "gilded age." It was a period of optimism and contradictions as the United States expanded both in size and in industrial development.

Stiff Victorian manners and dress codes prevailed, but the nation also fell in love with the unfettered lifestyle of the American cowboy.

The dream-girl symbol for the period was the "Gibson girl," created by illustrator Charles Dana Gibson. In contrast, the bawdy actress Lillie Langtry shocked theatergoers by appearing in pink tights. Shakespeare was so popular his plays were even performed in Western saloons.

Successful industrialists were the new American royalty. Lavish society balls and entertainments featured robust meals with many courses. Formal dinner menus were dictated either by French chefs at the White House or by Delmonico's and other expensive restaurants in New York City. However, for a brief period when Benjamin Harrison of Indiana was elected President, simpler, Midwestern-style food was in vogue in Washington.

In 1896, Fannie Farmer published her first cookbook. She was the first to call for carefully measured, "level" ingredients. Her *Boston Cooking School Cookbook* became one of the best sellers of all time. Another writer also became a household word when Dorothy Dix first published her "Advice to the Lovelorn."

Homesteaders raced to occupy the former Indian territories of Oklahoma and the Dakotas, and the new frontier states of Wyoming and Montana. European immigrants flooded into Ellis Island.

In February 1898, the U.S. battleship *Maine* was blown up in Havana Harbor. "Remember the *Maine*" became the cry of the Spanish-American War. Teddy Roosevelt's "Rough Riders" were the new American heroes.

Many Americans looked back on the 1890s as the "Gay Nineties". . . one of the happiest periods in American history. Thomas A. Edison's kinescope (motion pictures) was given first showings in New York. Inventions by Alexander Graham Bell and Henry Ford began to transform the country and the world. Average workers earned about $12 a week for 50 to 60 hours work. A quart of milk cost 6¢, and for 12¢ you could buy a pound of steak.

In the spring of 1889, Johns Hopkins, a Baltimore merchant, founded what was to become one of the nation's outstanding hospitals.

Although the business was planned in 1888, it was not until September 1889 that a man named Willoughby M. McCormick first began making fruit syrups in a basement in downtown Baltimore. The first site of McCormick & Company was at 33 Hanover Street, just north of Lombard.

Products were sold door-to-door by horse and buggy. Willoughby was not only the manufacturer but the entire sales force. From the beginning, his motto was "Make the Best—Someone Will Buy It."

From this modest beginning, the history of the world's largest producer of spices, seasonings and flavorings is interwoven with the story of the successful search for quality.

Special Pumpkin Pie (page 16)

1889

Nobel prize benefactor Alfred Nobel said, ''A good reputation is more important than a clean shirt. You can always wash a shirt, but not your reputation.''

On September 27, McCormick & Company was started in Baltimore, in one room and a cellar, by 25-year-old Willoughby M. McCormick and his staff of two girls and a boy. The address was 33 Hanover Street. First products were root beer, flavoring extracts and fruit syrups and juices. Other products sold under Bee Brand and Silver Medal trademarks: Iron Glue (''Sticks Everything But the Buyer'') and Uncle Sam's Nerve and Bone Liniment (''For Man or Beast''). Products were sold door-to-door; the new company's motto: ''Make the Best—Someone Will Buy It.''

The Johns Hopkins Hospital opened in Baltimore.

Invented at Antoine's Restaurant in New Orleans—named because of the richness of the sauce.

¾ *cup butter*
1   *10-ounce package frozen chopped spinach*
1 tablespoon Instant Minced Onion
1 teaspoon Parsley Flakes
½ *teaspoon Chervil Leaves*
⅛ *teaspoon Tarragon Leaves*
½ *teaspoon Bon Appétit®*
⅛ *teaspoon ground Red Pepper*
⅛ *teaspoon ground White Pepper*
Dash Instant Garlic Powder
2 tablespoons fine dry, unseasoned, bread crumbs
Rock salt
24 oysters on the half shell
Hollandaise Sauce (recipe below)

Melt butter in saucepan. Thaw and drain spinach. Add spinach to butter with next 8 ingredients. Simmer mixture 15 minutes. Remove from heat. Add bread crumbs. Make Hollandaise Sauce (recipe below). Spread layer of rock salt in shallow baking pan. Arrange oysters on salt. Spread 1 tablespoon of spinach mixture over each oyster. Top each with 1½ teaspoons Hollandaise Sauce. Broil 4 to 5 inches from heat 4 minutes. Serve oysters immediately.

Makes 24 Oysters Rockefeller

Hollandaise Sauce: In small saucepan, combine one 1.25-ounce package Hollandaise Sauce Mix, ⅛ teaspoon Tarragon Leaves, ⅛ teaspoon ground Mustard, and 1 tablespoon olive oil. Gradually stir in ¾ cup water, mixing well. Cook over medium heat, stirring constantly, until sauce thickens.

Makes ¾ cup sauce

OYSTER STEW

A dish that has changed little since the early days of oystering on the Chesapeake Bay. Remember the description of Oyster Stew as prepared by Big Jimbo, the cook aboard the *Jenny T.* in James Michener's book *Chesapeake*.

1 cup butter
2 quarts oysters, with liquid
½ teaspoon ground Black Pepper
2½ teaspoons Bon Appétit
1 tablespoon Worcestershire sauce
¼ teaspoon Instant Onion Powder
⅛ teaspoon Oregano Leaves
2 quarts milk
1 quart half-and-half or light cream

In 6-quart enamel or stainless steel kettle, melt butter. Add oysters with liquid and next 5 ingredients. Simmer 5 minutes, stirring occasionally. Stir in milk and cream. Heat slowly. Do not let stew boil.

QUICK AND EASY   *Makes 5 quarts*

Note: This recipe is easily halved or doubled, depending on the number of people to be served.

1890

The Company moved to larger quarters at 308 W. German Street. The following products were added to the line: lubricating and machine oils, witch hazel, blood purifier, cold cream, bay rum, toilet water, asafetida (a vile-smelling material hung around the neck to ward off illness), sulphur, epsom salts, borax, liver pills, castor oil, food colors, talcum powder, sulphate quinine, worm confections, cream of tartar, tooth powder, ammonia, quinine tablets, calomel tablets.

During the Victorian era, *nice* people referred to a chicken leg as the "first joint," and if you asked for the breast instead of "white meat," it was your hostess's moral obligation to faint.

Created in 1893 by Oscar of the Waldorf-Astoria Hotel in New York City.

2 cups cored, diced Red Delicious apples
2 cups cored, diced Yellow Delicious apples
½ cup chopped celery
½ cup raisins
½ cup chopped walnuts
1 cup mayonnaise
2 tablespoons sugar
⅛ teaspoon Apple Pie Spice
⅛ teaspoon pure Vanilla Extract
Lettuce cups

Place first 5 ingredients in mixing bowl. In small bowl, combine remaining ingredients except lettuce. Mix well. Pour over fruit. Toss gently to mix. Chill before serving. Serve in lettuce cups.

EASY
CAN DO AHEAD

Makes 5½ cups

1891

Roberdeau A. McCormick joined his brother, Willoughby, in the business.

1892

William Painter invented the crown cork bottle cap in Baltimore.

The first issue of the *Baltimore Afro-American* was published.

1893

The Johns Hopkins Medical School opened.

McCormick & Company moved to S. Howard Street.

An easy and luscious dessert created during the Age of Opulence—dramatic to prepare at the table.

> 1   *16½-ounce can pitted dark sweet cherries,*
> *in heavy syrup*
> *1 teaspoon Arrowroot*
> *1 teaspoon cold water*
> *⅛ teaspoon ground Cinnamon*
> *Dash ground Nutmeg*
> *½ cup brandy*
> *¼ cup Kirsch (cherry brandy)*
> *Vanilla ice cream*

Pour cherries and syrup into a small saucepan. Dissolve arrowroot in cold water. Add mixture to cherries along with cinnamon and nutmeg. Heat to a boil. Reduce heat and simmer 1 minute, stirring constantly. Remove from heat. In separate saucepan, heat brandy and Kirsch to lukewarm. Pour over cherries and CAREFULLY ignite. Serve sauce immediately over vanilla ice cream.

EASY   *Makes 2 cups sauce*

MICROWAVE DIRECTIONS

Use same ingredients, increasing amounts as indicated. Pour cherries and syrup into a medium microwavable bowl. Dissolve 2 teaspoons (increased from 1 teaspoon) arrowroot in 1½ teaspoons cold water (increased from 1 teaspoon). Add mixture to cherries along with cinnamon and nutmeg. Microcook, uncovered, on High 5 minutes, stirring after each minute. Pour brandy and Kirsch into a separate microwavable bowl. Microcook, uncovered, on 50% power (Medium) 1½ minutes. Pour over cherries and CAREFULLY ignite. Serve sauce immediately over vanilla ice cream.

QUICK AND EASY   *Makes 2 cups sauce*

1894

The first Maryland Hunt Cup race was held.

Bee Brand Roach Powder was added to the line and other products were gradually introduced to enlarge the line: bluing for laundry purposes, household ammonia, flypaper, roach traps, pest lamps, chicken powder, bird seed and gravel. Tradenames for original products were Wild Cherry Tonic, Uncle Sam's Horse and Cattle Powder and Death to Pain.

Brochures for Chicago's Columbian Exposition featured advertisements for Bee Brand Insect Powder, Omega Roach Powder, Iron Glue and root beer.

The Company exported goods overseas for the first time.

1895

Regular service of the first electric railway locomotive in the world, the Baltimore and Ohio Railroad, began.

The first Catholic college for women was founded—College of Notre Dame of Maryland.

Baseball's most famous player, Babe Ruth, was born in Baltimore.

The original corporation was dissolved and a partnership formed between Willoughby and Roberdeau McCormick.

Clover Brand was established for flavoring extracts, fruit syrups and juices. Bee Brand Tapioca and Mayonnaise were added to the line.

SPECIAL PUMPKIN PIE

1896

On September 15, the Company relocated to 44 S. Charles Street. Warehouse facilities were also opened at several downtown locations.

McCormick acquired F. G. Emmett Spice Company of Philadelphia. All equipment was shipped to Baltimore so the Company could enter the spice business.

The first McCormick cookbook was produced, and the first novelty premium was offered—the ''Little Puck Lamp,'' a perfume bottle, night lamp and toy combined.

Pastry for one-crust pie shell, 9-inch
2 eggs
1 16-ounce can pumpkin (2 cups)
½ cup brown sugar
1 teaspoon ground Cinnamon
¼ teaspoon ground Nutmeg
¼ teaspoon ground Ginger
¼ teaspoon ground Cloves
½ teaspoon salt
1 13-ounce can evaporated milk
Spiced Pecan Topping (recipe below)
Spiced Whipped Cream (recipe below)

Line a 9-inch pie plate with pastry. Beat eggs until light. Stir in pumpkin. Combine brown sugar with spices and salt. Stir into pumpkin mixture. Gradually stir in evaporated milk. Pour into pastry shell. Bake in 450°F. oven 15 minutes. Reduce temperature to 350°F. and bake 40 minutes longer. Cool. Sprinkle with Spiced Pecan Topping and decorate with spoonfuls of Spiced Whipped Cream.

Makes one 9-inch pie

(see photo page 10)

Spiced Pecan Topping: In large heavy skillet, mix 2 tablespoons brown sugar and 2 tablespoons butter with ⅛ teaspoon ground Cinnamon, ⅛ teaspoon ground Nutmeg and dash of ground Cloves. Heat, stirring, until sugar begins to melt. Quickly stir in 1 cup coarsely chopped pecans. Stir to coat nuts evenly with sugar. Cool.

Spiced Whipped Cream: Combine 1 cup whipping cream and 6 tablespoons confectioners' sugar. Add ¼ teaspoon ground Cinnamon, ⅛ teaspoon ground Nutmeg and ⅛ teaspoon ground Cloves. Beat cream mixture until stiff. Stir in 1 teaspoon pure Vanilla Extract.

SPICED CIDER

A popular drink way back then … as it is today.

1 gallon apple cider
1 cup orange juice
½ teaspoon Orange Extract
½ teaspoon Lemon Extract
4 3-inch pieces Cinnamon Stick
2 teaspoons whole Cloves
1 teaspoon whole Allspice

Combine all ingredients in large saucepan or Dutch oven. Cover. Heat to a boil. Reduce heat and simmer 45 minutes. Strain. Serve hot or cold.

EASY
CAN DO AHEAD

Makes 1 gallon

CARDINAL PUNCH

A frozen slush, served between courses at White House dinners during McKinley's administration.

1 48-ounce bottle cranberry juice cocktail
2 tablespoons lemon juice
2 cups light corn syrup
1 3-inch piece Cinnamon Stick
1 1-inch piece whole Ginger
2 whole Cardamom Seeds
1 Bay Leaf

Combine all ingredients in enamel or stainless steel kettle. Heat slowly and hold over low heat 10 minutes. Remove whole spices. Pour liquid into an 11 x 8 x 2-inch roasting pan. Freeze until solid. Remove from freezer. Scratch with tines of a fork until all of the mixture is broken into small flakes. Work quickly and return pan to freezer. To serve, pile frozen slush in sherbet glasses. Garnish with fresh mint. Serve between courses to refresh the palate, or as a refreshing, light dessert.

EASY
MUST DO AHEAD

Makes 8 cups

1897

The first country day school in the U.S., Gilman Country School (now Gilman School), opened in Maryland.

Bee Brand Spices and Mustard were added to the line.

1898

The Company leased 21 E. Lombard Street to use as a spice mill.

1899

Jockey Brand Livestock and Poultry Food were added to the line of products.

Turn of the Century

By the start of the twentieth century, the United States had become one of the greatest economic powers the world had ever known. Congress enacted the Pure Food and Drug Act. Carrie Nation, Kansas anti-saloon agitator, began raiding drinking establishments with a hatchet.

When President William McKinley was assassinated in 1901, Theodore Roosevelt succeeded him. This change gave birth to the ''Progressive Movement.'' Writers called ''muckrakers'' focused public attention on widespread corruption in business and government. Roosevelt decided to end favoritism toward these special interests and announced plans to give workers and farmers a ''Square Deal.'' By refusing to shoot a bear, Roosevelt launched America's favorite toy, the ''teddy bear.''

Meals of the era were elaborate. Dinners often had 8 to 12 courses. Menus often included game and such dishes as chicken croquettes and Lobster Newburg.

The Wright brothers successfully flew an airplane at Kitty Hawk, North Carolina in 1903. The U.S. signed a treaty to begin construction of the Panama Canal.

A 1904 fire in downtown Baltimore burned 36 hours, destroyed most of the business district, including McCormick & Company, and caused $80 million in damage. Two years later, an earthquake and fire ruined most of downtown San Francisco. The entire plant of A. Schilling and Company (which McCormick purchased in 1947 to establish a West Coast brand) was destroyed. Both companies took immediate steps to rebuild.

The first radio set was advertised in 1906 by the Electric Importing Company of New York. It cost $7.50.

George M. Cohan, Ruth St. Dennis, Alla Nazimova and Oscar Hammerstein were stars of the theater scene. But none received more notice than actress Miss Maude Adams, who made news by dashing about the country in an Oldsmobile steered by a stick. The first cross-country auto trip took 52 days.

The first perfect major league baseball game was pitched by Cy Young of the Boston Americans.

The first ''private baths'' were advertised by an Atlantic City hotel, which may have had something to do with the *Ladies' Home Journal*'s admonishment that ''women of good birth and breeding long ago discarded the use of perfumes, relying only on a daily bath and fresh linen for their aura.''

Jack London published *The Call of the Wild*. Robert Peary's expedition reached the North Pole. Ragtime was the music, and jazz was on its way.

Cheddar-Brie Cheese Soup (page 21)

MARYLAND CRAB SOUP

A Chesapeake Bay specialty known for its spicy vegetable base, rich with chunks of crabmeat. Best made with the backfin meat of the Blue Crab.

2 tablespoons butter
¼ cup finely chopped onion
¼ cup finely chopped celery
¼ cup finely chopped carrots
½ teaspoon ground Black Pepper
1 Bay Leaf
⅛ teaspoon ground Red Pepper
¼ teaspoon ground Mustard
⅛ teaspoon Thyme Leaves
1½ teaspoons Bon Appétit
1 28-ounce can whole tomatoes, chopped, in liquid
2 teaspoons Chicken Flavor Base
1 quart water
1 pound backfin crabmeat

Combine all ingredients except crabmeat. Heat to a boil, stirring occasionally. Reduce heat and simmer 15 minutes. Add crabmeat. Heat 5 minutes. Remove bay leaf.

EASY
CAN DO AHEAD

Makes seven 1-cup servings

MICROWAVE DIRECTIONS

Use same ingredients, reducing water as indicated. In large microwavable bowl, combine all ingredients except crabmeat, reducing water to 3 cups (from 4 cups). Microcook, covered, on High 10 minutes, stirring and rotating twice. Microcook, covered, on 50% power (Medium) 10 minutes. Add crabmeat. Microcook on 25% power (Low) 5 minutes. Remove bay leaf.

QUICK AND EASY

Makes seven 1-cup servings

¼ cup butter
¼ cup diced onion
¼ cup diced celery
2 tablespoons flour
2 teaspoons Chicken Flavor Base
1½ cups hot water
1½ cups milk
4 ounces Brie cheese, cut in cubes
8 ounces Cheddar cheese, grated
1 tablespoon Chablis (white wine)
¼ teaspoon Parsley Flakes
¼ teaspoon Paprika
¼ teaspoon Basil Leaves
Herbed Croutons (recipe below)

Melt butter in 2-quart saucepan. Add onion and celery. Sauté until tender. Stir in flour, using a wire whisk. Cook 3 minutes, stirring constantly. Combine chicken flavor base with water. Slowly add broth and milk to saucepan. Heat to boiling, stirring constantly. Lower heat and stir in remaining ingredients. Stir with wire whisk until cheese is melted. Simmer 5 minutes at low heat. Serve hot with Herbed Croutons.

Makes 1 quart soup

Herbed Croutons: Slice one-half loaf Italian bread in ½-inch slices. Trim crusts from bread. Cut slices in ½ x 1-inch pieces. Set aside. Melt ½ cup butter in skillet. Add ⅛ teaspoon Instant Garlic Powder, ⅛ teaspoon Instant Onion Powder, ½ teaspoon Basil Leaves and ½ teaspoon Marjoram Leaves. Sauté bread cubes in hot butter mixture, turning to brown all sides. Drain on paper towels. Serve on soup or salad.

Makes 1½ cups croutons

(see photo page 18)

Note: To vary crouton recipe, substitute ⅛ teaspoon each freeze-dried Chopped Chives, Tarragon Leaves and Thyme Leaves in place of other herbs.

1902

The Company acquired a four-story plant at Concord Street and W. Falls Avenue.

The Company secured Banquet Brand as a tradename for spices and mustards. The Banquet Brand trademark was a candelabrum.

Willoughby McCormick received a patent for a triangular glass bottle, which was used to package sulphate quinine. Previously, wooden bottles had been used for this product.

POTATO SALAD

12 to 15 medium-sized baking potatoes
½ cup thinly sliced celery
½ cup chopped onion
4 hard-cooked eggs, peeled and sliced
1 cup mayonnaise
1 cup dairy sour cream
1 teaspoon ground Mustard
¼ teaspoon ground Black Pepper
⅛ teaspoon ground Red Pepper
1 teaspoon whole Coriander Seed
1½ teaspoons Seasoning Salt
½ pound bacon, cut in 1-inch pieces, cooked and drained

Cook potatoes in skins. Cool slightly, peel, and cut in bite-size cubes. Add celery, onion and sliced eggs. Combine next 7 ingredients. Pour over potato mixture and toss lightly. Chill. Sprinkle with bacon just before serving.

EASY
CAN DO AHEAD

Makes 7 cups

CRUNCHY CHICKEN

½ cup butter
¼ teaspoon ground Black Pepper
½ teaspoon Instant Garlic Powder
½ teaspoon Instant Onion Powder
¼ teaspoon Oregano Leaves
¼ teaspoon Paprika
1¼ teaspoons Seasoning Salt
½ teaspoon Parsley Flakes
1 3-pound broiler/fryer chicken, cut in pieces
1 cup crushed corn flakes

Melt butter. Add next 7 ingredients. Coat chicken with butter mixture and roll in corn flakes. Place in large baking dish in single layer. Sprinkle any remaining butter and corn flakes over chicken. Bake in 350°F. oven 1 hour and 15 minutes.

QUICK AND EASY PREPARATION

Makes 6 pieces chicken

MARYLAND CRAB CAKES

The traditional Maryland specialty, best made with the backfin meat of the Blue Crab.

1 slice white bread
1 egg, beaten
1 tablespoon mayonnaise
1 teaspoon Parsley Flakes
½ teaspoon Bon Appétit
½ teaspoon salt
¼ teaspoon ground Mustard
⅛ teaspoon Basil Leaves
⅛ teaspoon ground Ginger
⅛ teaspoon ground Black Pepper
⅛ teaspoon ground Red Pepper
Dash ground Cloves
1 pound backfin crabmeat
Oil for frying

Remove crust from bread. Break bread into fine crumbs. Mix bread with next 11 ingredients. Let stand until bread dissolves. Combine with crabmeat. Toss gently. Shape into 8 cakes. Fry in hot oil in skillet or deep-fat fryer at 375°F. 4 minutes or until golden brown, or brush with melted butter and broil.

EASY
CAN DO AHEAD—COOK JUST BEFORE SERVING

Makes 8 crab cakes

Note: You may substitute 1 teaspoon Chesapeake Bay Style Seafood Seasoning for the 9 seasonings listed above.

1904

The Great Baltimore Fire destroyed major portions of the business section of Baltimore, including McCormick. Temporary quarters were opened and a new five-story building was erected on the old site.

The tea bag was invented by Thomas Sullivan in New York.

1905

Tea was added to the Bee Brand label products and the Clover Blossom name was established for spices and mustard.

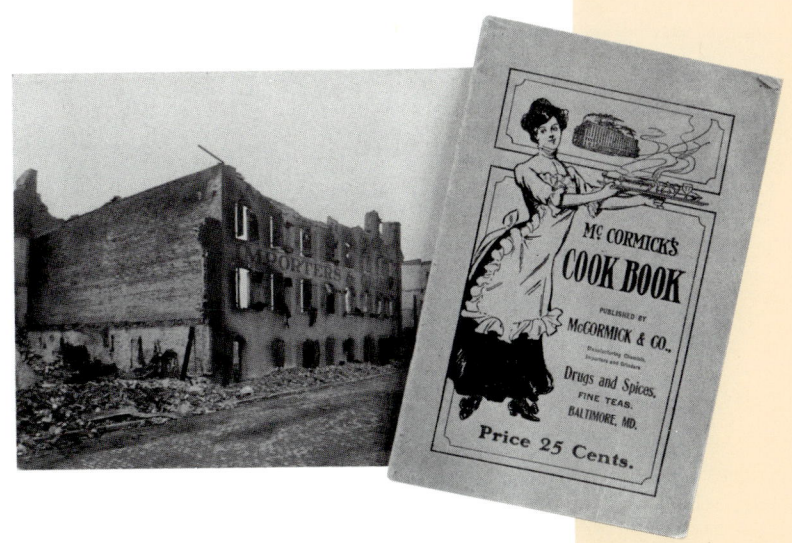

Carries well for picnics or brown bag lunches.

> 1 17.5-ounce package oatmeal-raisin cookie mix
> 1 teaspoon ground Cinnamon
> ⅛ teaspoon ground Nutmeg
> ⅛ teaspoon ground Cloves
> ½ cup chunky peanut butter
> 1 3-ounce package cream cheese, softened
> ¼ cup sugar
> 1 egg
> 2 tablespoons milk
> ½ teaspoon pure Vanilla Extract

In mixing bowl, combine first 4 ingredients. (*Note:* If mix contains 2 pouches, use both. If no pouch with liquid, add 2 tablespoons water.) Mix well. Reserve ½ cup for topping. Press remaining crumb mixture evenly into lightly greased 8 x 8 x 2-inch baking pan. Bake in 350°F. oven 5 minutes. In mixing bowl, combine last 6 ingredients and beat until creamy. Pour over crumb layer, spreading evenly. Sprinkle top with reserved crumb mixture. Bake in 350°F. oven 25 minutes. Cool. Cut into 1¼ x 1¾-inch bars.

EASY
FREEZES WELL

Makes twenty-four 1¼ x 1¾-inch bars

Note: May substitute chocolate chip or sugar cookie mix for oatmeal-raisin.

MICROWAVE DIRECTIONS

Use same ingredients. In mixing bowl, combine first 4 ingredients. (*Note:* If mix contains 2 pouches, use both. If no pouch with liquid, add 2 tablespoons water.) Mix well. Reserve ½ cup for topping. Press remaining crumb mixture evenly into an ungreased 8 x 8 x 2-inch microwavable baking dish. In ovens without turntables, place dish on upside down microwavable plate. Microcook, covered, on High 2 minutes, rotating once. Set aside. In mixing bowl, combine last 6 ingredients and beat until creamy. Pour over crumb layer, spreading evenly. Sprinkle top with reserved crumb mixture. Microcook, covered, on High 5 minutes, rotating twice. Remove from oven and let stand, covered, 5 minutes. Cut into 1¼ x 1¾-inch bars.

EASY
FREEZES WELL

Makes twenty-four 1¼ x 1¾-inch bars

SPICED ICED TEA

A refreshing and elegant summer beverage.

1 cup water
4 whole Cloves
3   3-inch pieces Cinnamon Stick
4 whole Allspice
1 teaspoon Mint Flakes
1 cup sugar
4 cups freshly brewed tea

Combine first 6 ingredients in saucepan. Heat to a boil, stirring until sugar dissolves. Cover. Reduce heat and simmer 20 minutes. Remove from heat and allow to cool. Strain. Combine tea with syrup. Serve over ice cubes in tall glasses.

EASILY DOUBLED OR TRIPLED

Makes 5 cups

Note: Syrup can be prepared ahead and refrigerated. The syrup portion may be used as a base for punch.

1909

Green Seal Salad Dressings and Table Relishes were added to the line of products.

The Walters Art Gallery opened at Charles and Centre Streets in Baltimore.

Period of World Conflict

Halley's Comet appeared as had been predicted in 1705. Many people panicked, believing that the earth would pass through the comet's tail and thus be destroyed.

A bitter split in the Republican Party swept Democrat Woodrow Wilson to victory as President. The Federal Reserve Act of 1913 established a national banking and currency system. That same year Congress set up the Department of Labor and created the Federal Trade Commission to handle complaints of unfair business practices. "Sweat shops" were outlawed in New York City.

The Boy Scouts of America was founded. The Panama Canal opened. The *Titanic* sank, and income tax became law. National attention was focused on the war sweeping Europe. American lives were lost when a German submarine sank the British liner *Lusitania*.

Finally, in 1917, after the Germans closed sea lanes to U.S. shipping and plots to sabotage American industries were uncovered, Wilson asked Congress to declare war. U.S. "doughboys" entered World War I, fighting "to make the world safe for democracy." The sub-machine gun was invented, and airplanes were used as strategic weapons in war to fight "dog fights." Wartime also made wrist watches popular for men. Song hits were "Over There" and "How Ya Gonna Keep 'Em Down on the Farm?"

Wartime shortages changed the nation's eating habits. Meals became less fancy and country food was popular.

At home, the National Park Service was established. Women began to smoke in public. Skyscrapers were allowed in New York City. Carl Sandburg published a collection of poems, *Chicago*.

Charlie Chaplin, at 27, became the highest-paid film star in the world with a contract for $675,000 a year. The Rose Bowl Game became a permanent feature of the "Tournament of Roses" in Pasadena, California. The Dixieland Jazz Band opened to sellout concerts in Chicago.

The 18th Amendment to the Constitution forbade the manufacture and sale of intoxicating liquors. The gangster era of bootleg whiskey began.

Salmon Mousse (page 28)

1910

McCormick became one of the first producers of tea in gauze pouches, thereby introducing "tea bags." Another popular consumer promotion was the Bee Brand Book of Gummed Labels for identifying homemade pickles, preserves, catsup and relishes.

The Flavoring Extracts Manufacturing Association was established with Willoughby McCormick as its first president. F.E.M.A. was started to establish the same standards of material and packaging throughout all the states and to improve the reputation of flavoring extract manufacturers.

French pilot Hubert Lathan made the first airplane flight over Baltimore to win a *Sunpapers* contest.

Black and Decker, largest producer of portable electric tools in the world, began operations in Baltimore.

1911

Lithographed tin canisters with friction plug closures were introduced by McCormick.

The 357-foot Bromo-Seltzer Tower, modeled after the Vecchio Palace in Florence, Italy, was completed in downtown Baltimore. The monument to Francis Scott Key was unveiled. The Women's Civic League held its first Flower Mart at Mt. Vernon Place.

Great party appetizer that must be prepared the day before.

½ cup water
1 envelope unflavored gelatine
2 tablespoons lemon juice
2 tablespoons Onion Flakes
½ cup mayonnaise
1 tablespoon prepared horseradish
2 teaspoons Dill Weed
½ teaspoon Bon Appétit
¼ teaspoon Paprika
1   15 or 16-ounce can salmon; drain and remove skin
1 cup whipping cream
Cucumbers

Lightly oil a 4-cup mold. In small saucepan, combine water and gelatine. Let stand 1 minute. Cook, stirring constantly over medium heat until gelatine is dissolved. Pour into food processor or blender. Add lemon juice and onion flakes. Cover. Blend at high speed 10 seconds. Add next 6 ingredients and blend about 30 seconds. Add whipping cream and blend at high speed until smooth. Pour into prepared mold. Cover and refrigerate until thick, at least 2 hours. Unmold and serve with sliced cucumbers.

MUST DO AHEAD   *Makes 4 cups*

(see photo page 26)

A fanciful and tasty salad developed by McCormick in 1913.

6 hard-cooked eggs
¼ teaspoon ground Mustard
½ teaspoon Seasoning Salt
⅛ teaspoon ground Black Pepper
¼ teaspoon Dill Weed
¼ cup mayonnaise
1 head lettuce
1 green pepper
1 large white onion

Shell eggs and cut in half, crosswise. Remove yolks and mash. Mix yolks with next 5 ingredients. Fill egg white halves with this mixture. Arrange lettuce cups on 6 salad plates. Cut green pepper in thin strips. Peel and slice onion. Cut onion slices in half and separate into strips. Arrange pepper and onion on lettuce. Place 2 egg halves in center. If desired, serve mayonnaise on the side.

EASY   *Makes 6 individual salads*

Note: Stuffed egg halves can be made a day ahead.

1912

Baltimore was host for the Democratic National Convention. Johns Hopkins alumnus Woodrow Wilson was nominated on the 46th ballot.

Alexander Edward Duncan created the Commercial Credit Corporation in Baltimore on $300,000 of borrowed capital.

The Company offered a 160-page manual of cookery for 50¢. Advertisements featured the slogan, "If it's Bee Brand, it's the best brand."

Willoughby's nephew, Charles P. McCormick, joined the Company as a part-time clerk in the shipping department.

1913

The Bee Brand Manual of Cookery was issued (called the "Blue Book of Culinary Art").

The British freighter *Alum Chine* exploded in Baltimore harbor, killing 33. It was the most serious peacetime sea disaster in Maryland history.

Immortalized by Owen Wister's 1906 novel, *Lady Baltimore*, this cake is worth the extra preparation time!

Cake:

6 egg whites, at room temperature
2 cups sugar
2½ cups sifted flour
1 tablespoon baking powder
½ teaspoon salt
1 cup butter
¾ cup milk
1 teaspoon Almond Extract

Beat egg whites until foamy. Gradually add ½ cup of the sugar, beating until stiff peaks form when beaters are lifted. Set aside. Sift together flour, baking powder and salt. Set aside. Cream butter with remaining 1½ cups sugar. Gradually add milk, alternating with sifted dry ingredients. Add almond extract. Beat well. Scrape bowl. Beat mixture at medium speed 3 minutes longer. Fold in reserved beaten egg whites. Pour into three greased and floured 8-inch layer cake pans. Bake in 375°F. oven 30 to 35 minutes or until cake tests done. Cool in pans on wire rack 5 minutes. Turn out on racks. Cool.

Makes three 8-inch layers

Frosting:

1½ cups sugar
¼ teaspoon salt
¼ cup water
3 egg whites, at room temperature
¼ teaspoon Cream of Tartar
3 tablespoons light corn syrup
¼ teaspoon Almond Extract
1 cup chopped pecans
1 cup chopped raisins
½ cup finely chopped dried figs

In double-boiler top over simmering water, beat together first 6 ingredients. With mixer at high speed, beat until frosting forms soft peaks when beaters are lifted, about 7 minutes. Remove from heat. Add almond extract. Continue beating until mixture forms stiff peaks, scraping sides occasionally. Add remaining ingredients. Stir to mix well. Do not use electric mixer. Spread frosting between layers and on sides and top of cake.

Frosts one 8-inch layer cake

1916

The Baltimore Symphony Orchestra presented its first program.

The federal income tax was ruled constitutional, and interstate shipment of goods manufactured by children under 14 was forbidden.

A British seaman saw a bottle bobbing in the North Atlantic. It was the final message sent from the *Lusitania* before it sank, taking with it some 1,198 passengers.

An elegant, old-fashioned dessert that takes time but should be made a day ahead. This makes a beautiful presentation for a dinner party.

2 **10-ounce packages frozen raspberries in syrup**
24 to 30 ladyfingers
1 cup milk
2 egg yolks
2 envelopes unflavored gelatine
1 cup sugar
¼ teaspoon salt
½ teaspoon pure Vanilla Extract
2 egg whites
¼ cup sugar
1 cup whipping cream
6 tablespoons confectioners' sugar
Optional: Sweetened whipped cream

Thaw raspberries. Line a 2½-quart Charlotte mold or soufflé dish with ladyfingers. Scald milk. Beat egg yolks. Combine gelatine, sugar and salt. Mix well. Stir egg yolks and gelatine mixture into hot milk. Cook over low heat, stirring until gelatine is dissolved. Press raspberries through a fine strainer to make 1½ cups juice and pulp. Discard seeds. Stir raspberry purée and vanilla into gelatine mixture. Chill until partially set. Beat egg whites until foamy. Gradually add sugar, beating until soft peaks form when beaters are lifted. Whip cream with confectioners' sugar. Fold egg whites and whipped cream into gelatine mixture. Pour into mold. Chill at least 4 hours or overnight. Loosen edge with a knife or small spatula. Invert serving plate over mold. Invert mold with plate. Shake sharply two or three times. Remove mold. If desired, decorate with sweetened whipped cream.

MUST DO AHEAD   *Makes 10 generous slices*

PROHIBITION PUNCH

A non-alcoholic punch, reminiscent of the Prohibition era. A flavorful alternative to iced tea.

4 quarts water
½ cup sugar
10 whole Cloves
2   3-inch pieces Cinnamon Stick
8 whole Allspice
1 whole Nutmeg
4 whole Cardamom Seeds
8 McCormick Tea Bags
1 quart clear apple juice
1 cup white grape juice

Combine 1 quart water, sugar and spices. Heat to a boil. Reduce heat and simmer 10 minutes. Remove spices. Heat 1 quart water to a boil. Pour over tea bags and steep 5 minutes. Combine spiced mixture, tea, remaining 2 quarts water and juices. Stir well. Serve over ice cubes. Garnish with slices of Red and Yellow Delicious apples or lemon wedges.

QUICK AND EASY
CAN DO AHEAD

Makes 1 gallon

1918

"Baltimore's Own" 313th Regiment helped take the French town of Montfaucon, a vital German stronghold, in World War I.

Fragroma, a food-flavoring extract, and San-Tay, a laxative, were added to the line of products.

1919

"The Bee Brand Perfect Products" advertising campaign focused on 16 of the Company's most popular products and featured a Scotch lass and laddie as trade figures.

McCormick announced a new building project on Light and Barre Streets.

Resoleums, spices, food flavors and Fruitall maltless flavors and extracts were added to the product line.

The Roar and Crash of the Twenties

The U.S. Senate refused to ratify the League of Nations' covenant. Stock speculation, reckless spending and real estate booms sent prices skyrocketing. The era of the "flaming youth" rebelled against Puritan standards of the pre-war years. Henry Ford's Model T put Americans behind the wheel.

Styled by John Held, "flappers" wore cloche hats, short skirts, bobbed hair and rolled-down stockings, smoked cigarettes, swallowed goldfish and drank bathtub gin in "speakeasies." Canned foods, ready-made clothing and new household appliances freed women, who by now had finally won the right to vote. The first licensed radio broadcast took place in 1920.

Baltimore-born and educated Emily Price Post wrote her first book of etiquette in 1922. It quickly became the last word in social conduct. Cooking at the table in chafing dishes was considered stylish.

Commander Richard E. Byrd became the first man to fly over the North Pole. Gertrude Ederle was the first woman to swim the English Channel. Charles A. Lindbergh's 33-hour solo flight across the Atlantic thrilled the nation and the world.

In Dayton, Tennessee, Clarence Darrow and William Jennings Bryan, two of the nation's best-known attorneys, debated whether the Bible or modern science offered the truth of mankind's creation. Scores of newsmen covered the so-called "monkey trial," including Baltimore's H. L. Mencken, whose reporting of the trial in 1925 became a classic of American journalism.

American literature flourished with such writers as Willa Cather, F. Scott Fitzgerald, Ernest Hemingway and Sinclair Lewis. Americans danced the Charleston and the Tango and rushed to hear John Barrymore speak for the first time on screen in the movie *Don Juan*. Al Jolson sang in *The Jazz Singer*. George Gershwin wrote "Rhapsody in Blue."

In 1927, Baltimore-born Babe Ruth hit 60 home runs to lead the Yankees' "Murderers' Row."

The future looked bright when Herbert Hoover became President in 1929. But in October the country suffered the worst business crash in its history. Banks failed. Millions of people lost everything they owned. Stores and factories closed, and the entire country seemed to be paralyzed . . . even the bootleggers!

In Chicago that same year, six members of the Moran gang were lined up against a wall and shot gangland style. That act became known as the St. Valentine's Day massacre.

Drunken Chicken (page 39)

1920

Banquet Salad Dressing, Mayonnaise Dressing and Mustard Dressing were added.

The Company employed a welfare worker to reduce expenses caused by lack of proper medical attention.

1921

A new home for the House of McCormick opened on Light Street at the Baltimore harbor. The nine-story building had 12½ acres of sunlit floor space, its own railroad siding, a printing plant, analytical laboratory, machine shop, assembly hall, first aid room and a cafeteria which served hot lunch for 15¢ to 25¢.

Over 800 products were offered by the Company. A sifter top for Bee Brand Insect Powder was first used and Oriola Syrups and Extracts for maltless drinks were added to the product line.

4 teaspoons Chicken Flavor Base
1 quart water
1 teaspoon Instant Minced Onion
1 teaspoon Bon Appétit
⅛ teaspoon ground Black Pepper
1 cup mashed, cooked sweet potatoes
1 cup ½-inch diced, cooked sweet potatoes
1 tablespoon butter
¼ pound scallops, cut in ¼-inch pieces

Combine first 6 ingredients. Heat, stirring occasionally. Simmer 10 minutes. Add diced sweet potatoes. Hold over low heat. Melt butter. Sauté scallops 5 minutes. Add to soup.

EASY   *Makes 6 cups*

Note: Good use for leftover sweet potatoes.

Ginger

1922

Henry A. Berliner made the first helicopter flight, rising to a height of seven feet at College Park, Maryland.

A refrigeration plant was installed in the McCormick building to provide iced drinking water for the employees.

Baltimore Stadium opened with a football game between the Third Army and the Quantico Marines.

Kil-Spray, an insecticide, was added to the products.

Intrigue your guests with this variation on traditional cream of chicken soup.

1   *2½ to 3-pound whole broiler/fryer chicken*
2 teaspoons Parsley Flakes
6 cups water
1 Bay Leaf
¼ teaspoon Thyme Leaves
2 teaspoons Instant Minced Onion
6 tablespoons butter
6 tablespoons flour
2 cups half-and-half or light cream
1½ teaspoons Bon Appétit
1 tablespoon Chicken Flavor Base
¼ teaspoon ground White Pepper
½ cup popcorn, popped as desired,
following package directions

Wash chicken. Place in Dutch oven or large stockpot. Add 1 teaspoon of the parsley flakes and the next 4 ingredients. Heat to a boil. Reduce heat, cover, and simmer 35 to 40 minutes or until chicken is tender. Remove chicken from stock. Strain and reserve 4 cups stock. Cool. Remove meat from bones. Cut meat in ½-inch cubes. Melt butter over low heat in Dutch oven or 4-quart pot. Gradually add flour, stirring constantly until smooth. Cook over medium heat until bubbly. Gradually add 4 cups of reserved, strained chicken stock, stirring constantly. Add next 4 ingredients and remaining 1 teaspoon parsley flakes. Cook, stirring constantly, over medium heat until mixture begins to boil. Reduce heat and simmer 1 minute. Add chicken. Cook over low heat 2 minutes. Ladle soup into serving dishes. Top with popped popcorn. Serve immediately.

Makes 8 cups

DRUNKEN CHICKEN

Chicken in a rich rum sauce.

4 half chicken breasts, boneless, skinless
¼ cup light rum
¼ teaspoon ground Nutmeg
1 tablespoon soy sauce
1 tablespoon lime juice
1 tablespoon brown sugar
¾ teaspoon Bon Appétit
¼ teaspoon crushed Red Pepper
⅛ teaspoon ground Ginger
2 tablespoons butter
2 cups sliced mushrooms
1 cup dairy sour cream

Pound chicken breasts to ½-inch thickness. Pierce several times, using tines of a fork. Place in single layer in shallow glass dish. Set aside. Combine next 8 ingredients. Mix well. Pour liquid over chicken. Marinate at room temperature 30 minutes, turning once. Melt butter in skillet over medium heat. Reserving marinade, remove chicken and sauté in butter. Remove chicken. Keep warm. Sauté mushrooms. Reduce heat and add marinade. Gradually add sour cream. Stir to blend. Cook, covered, over low heat 5 minutes. Serve sauce over chicken breasts. Sprinkle with additional nutmeg if desired.

EASY   *Makes 4 servings of ½ chicken breast with sauce*

(see photo page 34)

1923

Group life insurance was added to employees' benefits. Annual employee physicals were begun, and a nurse made home calls to those who were ill.

1924

Jellex, a jelly-making material, was added to products.

Editors H. L. Mencken and George Jean Nathan began their collaboration in Baltimore on the *American Mercury Magazine,* a forum for literary expression and social criticism.

The Company established the cost system department.

Modified from the *McCormick Bee Brand Cookbook* version. During the 1920s, this recipe would have been prepared in a chafing dish. Today we have our choice of the electric skillet or the microwave oven!

2 tablespoons fine dry, unseasoned, bread crumbs
1 egg, beaten
¼ teaspoon ground Black Pepper
½ teaspoon Seasoning Salt
1 teaspoon Instant Minced Onion
½ teaspoon Parsley Flakes
1 pound ground beef
1   0.87-ounce package Brown Gravy Mix
¼ teaspoon Marjoram Leaves
2 tablespoons dry wine (red or white)

Mix bread crumbs with next 5 ingredients. Gently mix with ground beef. Shape into 5 patties. Flatten slightly. In skillet, brown patties on each side over medium heat. Drain excess fat. Prepare gravy following package directions. Add marjoram and dry wine. Pour gravy over patties in skillet. Cook, covered, over low heat 5 minutes.

QUICK AND EASY   *Makes 5 patties with sauce*

 MICROWAVE DIRECTIONS

Use same ingredients, reducing wine as indicated. Combine first 6 ingredients. Gently mix with ground beef. Shape into 5 patties. Flatten slightly. In microwavable 10-inch pie plate, arrange patties in a circular pattern. Microcook, covered, on High 3 to 4 minutes, turning patties over and rotating once. Remove from oven and let stand, covered, 2 minutes. Drain liquid. To prepare gravy, place contents of packet in a small microwavable bowl. Gradually stir in 1 cup cold water. Stir in marjoram and 1 tablespoon dry wine (reduced from 2 tablespoons). Microcook, uncovered, on High 3 to 4 minutes, stirring at end of each minute. Pour gravy over patties in pie plate. Microcook, covered, on 50% power (Medium) 2 to 3 minutes, rotating once. Remove from oven and let stand 2 minutes before serving.

QUICK AND EASY   *Makes 5 patties with sauce*

1925

Baltimore-born heartthrob Francis X. Bushman starred as Messala in the movie *Ben-Hur.*

The Company offered a *Drawing and Tracing Book* for children which featured the countries of origin of various raw materials used in Bee and Banquet Brand products.

C. P. McCormick was elected to the Board of Directors.

CREAMED ASPARAGUS

A seasonal favorite from the chafing dish era.

2 pounds fresh asparagus
3 tablespoons butter
2 tablespoons flour
2 teaspoons Bon Appétit
⅛ teaspoon ground Coriander
¼ teaspoon ground White Pepper
⅛ teaspoon Italian Seasoning
1 cup whipping cream
1 cup milk

Wash asparagus. Peel thick part of stems. Steam asparagus until tender. Cool slightly. Cut in 2-inch pieces. Melt butter. Stir in flour and next 4 ingredients. Cook, stirring constantly, 2 to 3 minutes. Gradually stir in whipping cream and milk. Cook, stirring, until sauce thickens slightly. Add asparagus pieces. Cook 1 minute.

Makes 2 cups sauce
(4 to 6 servings with asparagus)

Note: Sauce can be used to prepare any creamed vegetable.

A chafing dish specialty, very popular in the twenties for Sunday supper. Derives its name from the wonderful Welsh sense of humor—the hunter who returned empty-handed sat down to a tasty cheese dish that came to be known as Welsh ''Rabbit.''

1 pound Cheddar cheese, shredded
1 tablespoon butter
1 cup milk or beer
½ teaspoon Bon Appétit
½ teaspoon Paprika
Dash ground Red Pepper
½ teaspoon ground Mustard
1 egg, beaten
Toast or saltine crackers

In top of double boiler or chafing dish over boiling water, melt cheese with butter. Gradually stir in milk or beer. Add next 4 ingredients. Stir to mix well. Stir in beaten egg. Serve over toast or crackers.

QUICK AND EASY   *Makes 3 cups*

½ teaspoon ground Ginger
1 teaspoon ground Mustard
1 teaspoon Almond Extract
1 tablespoon lemon juice
¼ cup dark brown sugar, packed
½ cup chili sauce
2 tablespoons dry wine (red or white)
1   18-ounce jar baked beans
1 medium-size onion

In a 1½ to 2-quart bowl, combine first 7 ingredients, mixing well. Stir in beans. Pour half the mixture in buttered 1½-quart baking dish. Slice onion and separate into rings and place over beans. Top with remaining beans. Cover and bake in 350°F. oven 1 hour.

EASY
CAN DO AHEAD

Makes 2½ cups

MICROWAVE DIRECTIONS

Omit wine and reduce ingredients as indicated. In a 1½-quart microwavable dish, combine first 6 ingredients, reducing extract to ½ teaspoon (from 1 teaspoon), lemon juice to 1 teaspoon (from 1 tablespoon) and chili sauce to ¼ cup (from ½ cup). Omit wine. Mix well. Stir in beans. Slice onion, separate into rings, and place over beans. Microcook, covered, on High 5 minutes, stirring and rotating once. Microcook, covered, on 50% power (Medium) 5 minutes. Remove from oven, uncover, and let stand 5 minutes.

QUICK AND EASY

Makes 2½ cups

1928

The *Graf Zeppelin* sailed above Baltimore at the end of its first voyage across the Atlantic.

The Hippodrome in Baltimore was one of the country's biggest movie theaters, averaging 30,000 spectators weekly.

The Flag House was dedicated as a national shrine in Baltimore.

McCormick sales hit the $5 million mark—and C. P. McCormick was named Vice President.

The first traffic-actuated signal in the world was installed in Baltimore. Charles Adler, Jr., was the inventor.

Red Arrow Insecticide was added to the products.

The Company established an in-house newsletter called *The Bee*.

New packaging was introduced which featured a blue diagonal band to identify the package as either Bee Brand or McCormick's.

4 large sweet potatoes
½ cup water
⅓ cup butter
½ cup dark brown sugar
¼ cup chopped walnuts
¾ teaspoon pure Vanilla Extract
¼ teaspoon Pumpkin Pie Spice
⅛ teaspoon Lemon Peel
¼ cup dark corn syrup

Wash potatoes. Place in large saucepan or Dutch oven. Cover with water. Heat to a boil. Reduce heat, cover, and simmer until tender, about 25 to 30 minutes. Drain and cool. Peel and quarter. Place in buttered 13 x 9 x 2-inch baking dish. Set aside. Combine remaining ingredients in small saucepan. Simmer 5 minutes. Pour sauce over potatoes. Bake, uncovered, in 375°F. oven 50 minutes, basting with sauce several times.

CAN DO AHEAD   *Makes 5 cups*

Note: You can use sauce portion with drained, canned sweet potatoes.

 MICROWAVE DIRECTIONS

Use same ingredients, changing amounts as indicated. Use 4 medium-size sweet potatoes (2½ x 5 inches). Wash potatoes. Prick potatoes over entire surface, using tines of a fork. Place potatoes in circular pattern on microwave oven floor. Microcook, uncovered, on High 12 to 15 minutes, rotating every 4 minutes. Let stand 8 minutes. Peel and quarter. Place in a microwavable 9-inch pie plate. Set aside. Combine remaining ingredients in medium microwavable bowl, reducing water to ¼ cup (from ½ cup). Microcook, uncovered, on High 4 to 6 minutes, stirring twice. Pour sauce over potatoes. Microcook, uncovered, on 50% power (Medium) 8 to 10 minutes, rotating plate and basting potatoes with sauce several times.

CAN DO AHEAD   *Makes 3½ to 4 cups*

2 cups milk
6 tablespoons maple syrup
¼ cup finely chopped walnuts
4 eggs
⅓ cup sugar
¼ teaspoon salt
¾ teaspoon imitation Maple Flavor
1⁄16 teaspoon ground Nutmeg
⅛ teaspoon ground Cinnamon

Scald milk and set aside. Put 1 tablespoon maple syrup in each of six 6-ounce custard cups. Sprinkle 2 teaspoons walnuts over syrup in each cup. Set aside. In medium bowl, combine eggs, sugar and salt. Beat well. Stir in scalded milk, extract, nutmeg and cinnamon. Blend well. Pour mixture into custard cups, dividing evenly among the 6 custard cups. Set cups in baking pan. Pour hot water in pan to depth of 1 inch. Bake in 350°F. oven 40 minutes or just until a knife inserted 1 inch from edge comes out clean. Remove from oven. Let cool. Refrigerate overnight. To serve, loosen custard around edges and invert over serving plate. Shake to loosen custard.

MUST DO AHEAD   *Makes six 6-ounce custards*

1929

In its hometown, the Company opened the Banquet Tea Room at 217 W. Saratoga Street.

Black Arrow Insecticide was added to the products.

"The Arthur Godfrey Radio Show" began broadcasting from Baltimore.

The first computer was developed in Cambridge, Massachusetts, at M.I.T.

 ## MICROWAVE DIRECTIONS

Use same ingredients. Pour the milk into a 1-quart microwavable measuring cup. Microcook, uncovered, on 50% power (Medium) 5 to 6 minutes or until scalded. Put 1 tablespoon maple syrup in each of six 6-ounce microwavable custard cups. Sprinkle 2 teaspoons walnuts over syrup in each cup. Set aside. In medium bowl, combine remaining ingredients. Beat well. Stir in scalded milk. Blend well. Pour mixture into custard cups, dividing evenly among the 6 custard cups. Arrange cups in circular pattern on oven base. Microcook, uncovered, on 50% power (Medium) 8 to 10 minutes or until custard is set. Rotate cups occasionally during cooktime. Remove from oven and cool to room temperature. Refrigerate overnight. To serve, loosen custard around edges and invert over serving plate. Shake to loosen custard.

MUST DO AHEAD   *Makes six 6-ounce custards*

The Depression Years

"The Star-Spangled Banner," based on a poem about Fort McHenry and written by Francis Scott Key, was officially declared the national anthem.

For the first time, the U.S. government assumed the responsibility of rescuing the economy by active intervention in business. Franklin D. Roosevelt won the Presidency by advocating a "New Deal" for all Americans and by reminding them that "the only thing we have to fear is fear itself." His "fireside chats" marked the first regular use of the medium of radio by a Chief Executive.

Recovery was the goal, but the Depression persisted. Dust bowls in the Midwest contributed to the ruination of homesteaders. Enactment of a Federal Emergency Relief Act and creation of the Works Progress Administration and Civilian Conservation Corps helped put people back to work.

Other emergency acts established the Tennessee Valley Authority and permitted the President to reopen banks. A minimum wage of 40¢ an hour was established with time-and-a-half pay for work over 44 hours a week. Congress also passed social security laws. Government spending for social welfare programs rose 1,000%.

The Associated Press picked the Top Ten Football Teams for the first time. At the top was Minnesota. Amelia Earhart became the first woman to fly alone across the Atlantic Ocean. Radio City Music Hall was opened.

Headlining all news events was the abdication of King Edward VIII of England for "the woman I love," Wallis Warfield Simpson of Baltimore, Maryland.

A Halloween radio show by Orson Welles called "War of the Worlds" seemed so real it caused nationwide panic. Electric refrigerators replaced ice boxes and recipes for freezer tray ice cream came into vogue.

Clark Gable won the Academy Award for *It Happened One Night*. Shirley Temple dolls and Hollywood stars were major topics of the day, with millions of people attending movies to win dishes and talent contests. *Gone With the Wind* was the book of the decade. The nationwide search for someone to play Scarlett O'Hara had even young girls in New York City practicing Georgia drawls.

Like Wilson, Roosevelt watched the storm clouds of war begin. Germany turned to Nazism, Italy to Fascism, and Japan marched into China. When Hitler seized Czechoslovakia in 1939, many Americans awakened from their comfortable isolationism to the reality of another world war.

Corn Salad in Pepper Shells (page 49)

A taste of the old South, this is an excellent use for end-of-the-season tomatoes.

4 large, slightly underripe tomatoes
¼ cup fine dry, unseasoned, bread crumbs
½ cup flour
1 teaspoon Seasoning Salt
½ teaspoon ground Black Pepper
¼ teaspoon Thyme Leaves
⅛ teaspoon ground Red Pepper
1 egg beaten with 1 tablespoon water
Butter

Wash tomatoes and remove stems. Cut each tomato in three thick slices. Combine bread crumbs with next 5 ingredients. Mix well. Dip tomato slices in egg mixture, then roll in crumb mixture. Sauté in melted butter over medium heat, turning once, to lightly brown both sides. Serve hot.

QUICK AND EASY   *Makes 12 tomato slices*

1930

F. Scott Fitzgerald wrote, "Baltimore is very nice and with plenty of cousins and Princetonians."

McCormick offices opened in Houston and San Francisco.

Monopoly®, a Parker Brothers board game, was introduced.

1931

Through an act of Congress, "The Star-Spangled Banner" officially became the national anthem.

Henry Walters bequeathed his art gallery to the city of Baltimore.

Best-selling spices at this time were cinnamon, black pepper, mustard, cake spice, paprika and ginger.

The first nighttime outdoor polo game was played.

The Board of Directors announced a five-day week. The Company would be closed on Saturdays and Sundays.

A different, delicious way to serve corn at any time of the year.

4 green peppers
⅓ cup salad oil
½ teaspoon ground Mustard
½ teaspoon ground Black Pepper
⅛ teaspoon ground Red Pepper
1 tablespoon Instant Minced Onion
2 tablespoons vinegar
3 cups (two 10.5-ounce cans) whole kernel corn
1 6-ounce jar pimiento, cut in 1-inch squares
1 cup thinly sliced celery
1 8-ounce can water chestnuts, thinly sliced

Cut tops from green peppers and remove seeds. Cut top edge in petal shape, if desired. Parboil in boiling water 5 minutes. Mix next 6 ingredients. Combine corn, pimiento, celery and water chestnuts. Add dressing. Toss to mix well. Fill peppers with corn mixture. Chill, covered.

QUICK AND EASY
MUST DO AHEAD

Makes 4 servings, 1 filled pepper each

(see photo page 46)

1932

The Bee Brand Insecticide advertising campaign reached 30 million Americans through 185 newspapers and farm papers.

The Company introduced tea bags made of cellophane and a newly designed, pyramid-shaped extract bottle.

Bee Brand Insecticide Shampoo, Soap and Powder were added products.

The first issue of a new in-house newsletter, *Bee Lines*, came out.

Willoughby McCormick died on November 4, and 36-year-old C. P. McCormick was elected President and Chairman of the Board. Faced with the serious crisis of the Depression, he quickly implemented a new business philosophy called Multiple Management, which encouraged employee participation. A Junior Board of Directors was established.

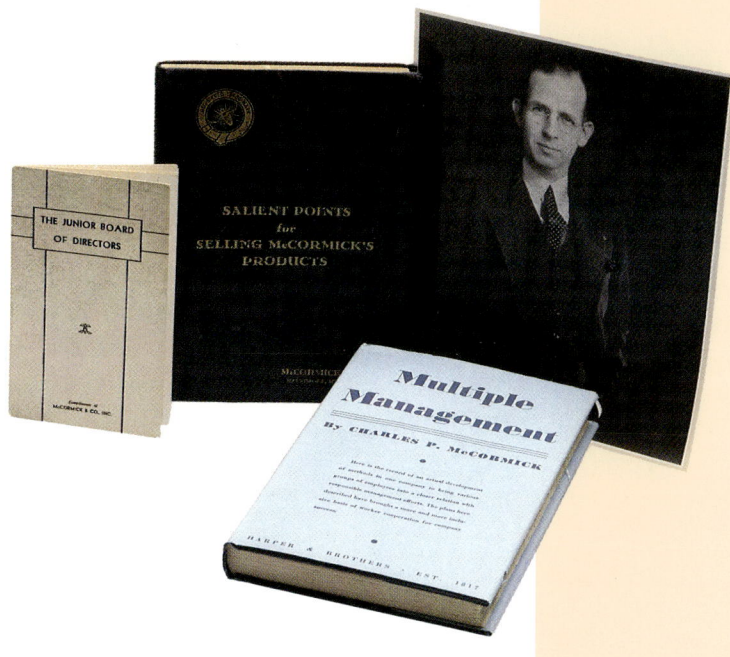

1932

The first meeting of the new Junior Executives was called by C. P. on November 23 ''to meet and discuss the problems of business.''

The President's Award was started— a gold pin with Bee Brand on it. One was given in recognition of performance, cheerfulness and ''the Two for One Spirit.'' This award later became the C. P. McCormick Award.

The Company began working on a new wage scale based on a 40-hour week and an increase in pay.

The open door policy was started. C. P. was available at all times for those who wished to speak with him.

The Company began giving each employee a turkey at Thanksgiving.

The blender was invented in this decade, making many kitchen chores easier.

3 egg yolks
2 tablespoons lemon juice
¼ teaspoon Seasoning Salt
¼ teaspoon Thyme Leaves
¼ teaspoon Instant Minced Onion
⅛ teaspoon ground Mustard
Dash ground Red Pepper
½ cup butter

Place first 7 ingredients in blender jar. Cover. Blend at top speed 2 seconds. Cut butter into pieces and heat until foaming. Remove feeder cap from blender cover. Blend at top speed. Add hot butter very slowly in a thin stream of droplets. Serve over asparagus or broccoli.

EASY   *Makes ¾ cup*

SPOONBREAD

A moist, fluffy corn bread, Southern cousin to a soufflé.

¾ cup yellow cornmeal
2¼ cups milk
1   17-ounce can whole kernel corn
½ cup melted butter
1 cup flour
1 teaspoon Seasoning Salt
¼ teaspoon Thyme Leaves
¼ teaspoon ground Red Pepper
2 tablespoons sugar
2 teaspoons baking powder
4 eggs, beaten

In stainless steel bowl over boiling water, combine cornmeal and milk. Stir until smooth. Cook, stirring occasionally, 10 minutes. Stir in corn and melted butter. Mix flour with next 5 ingredients. Stir into corn mixture. Stir in beaten eggs. Pour into greased 9-inch square baking pan or a 9-inch cast iron skillet. Bake in 350°F. oven 45 to 50 minutes. Serve hot in pan. Use a large spoon to scoop out servings.

Makes one 9-inch square or round

HERB BISCUITS

Quick drop biscuits—also makes good dumplings.

2 cups biscuit mix
¼ teaspoon Marjoram Leaves
¼ teaspoon Oregano Leaves
½ teaspoon Thyme Leaves
¼ teaspoon Instant Onion Powder
1 cup milk

Combine biscuit mix with next 4 ingredients. Stir in milk. Drop from spoon to make 10 equal biscuits, on lightly greased baking sheet. Bake in 425°F. oven 12 to 15 minutes or until lightly browned. Serve hot.

QUICK AND EASY
FREEZES WELL

Makes 10 biscuits

Aromatic and flavorful, with a fine velvety grain.

½ cup vegetable shortening
¼ cup sugar
1 egg, beaten
½ cup dark molasses
1¾ cups sifted flour
1 teaspoon baking soda
1 teaspoon ground Ginger
½ teaspoon ground Cinnamon
½ teaspoon ground Cloves
½ teaspoon salt
½ cup milk
Spicy Brown Sugar Hard Sauce (recipe below)

Cream together first 2 ingredients. Add egg and molasses. Beat well. Sift together next 6 ingredients. Add dry ingredients alternately with milk to creamed mixture. Blend well. Pour into greased 8 x 8 x 2-inch baking pan. Bake in 350°F. oven 30 to 35 minutes or until cake tests done. Serve warm with Spicy Brown Sugar Hard Sauce.

Makes 6 servings, 3½ x 2⅔ inches each

Spicy Brown Sugar Hard Sauce: Soften 1½ cups butter at room temperature. Add ¼ teaspoon ground Nutmeg, 1 teaspoon pure Vanilla Extract, ¼ teaspoon ground Cinnamon, ⅛ teaspoon ground Cloves, 1 pound light brown sugar and 1 tablespoon light cream. Beat with electric mixer until very light and fluffy, about 10 minutes. Refrigerate in covered container. Serve on hot gingerbread or plum pudding.

CAN DO AHEAD
FREEZES WELL

Makes 3½ cups

ORIGINAL STYLE
CHOCOLATE CHIP COOKIES

In the style of the all-time American favorite invented at the Toll House Inn.

1 cup butter, softened
½ cup sugar
1 cup brown sugar
1 teaspoon pure Vanilla Extract
2 eggs
2¼ cups sifted flour
⅛ teaspoon ground Cinnamon
1 teaspoon baking soda
1 teaspoon salt
1 cup chopped walnuts
2   4-ounce packages German's sweet chocolate,
cut in ¾-inch squares

In large bowl, combine first 4 ingredients. Beat until creamy. Add eggs. Sift together next 4 ingredients. Gradually add dry ingredients to butter mixture. Mix well. Stir in walnuts and chocolate squares. Drop by rounded teaspoonfuls onto greased cookie sheets. Bake in 350°F. oven 8 to 10 minutes or until golden brown. Cool on wire rack.

CAN DO AHEAD
FREEZES WELL

Makes 4½ dozen cookies,
approximately 2½ inches in diameter

1935

The Company offered $1,000 to anyone who could show a competing product line as high in quality throughout or as profitable to the merchant.

The Sales Board was established.

SCREW TOP
No broken corks
. . . never drips

FINGER GRIPS
Easier to hold
can't slip

WIDER BASE
Stands up it
won't

IT'S THE FLAVOR THAT COUNTS!

For a delicious, mellow-rich vanilla flavor, try Bee Brand Vanilla Extract. Made always from choicest Mexican vanilla beans. More than pure. Its quality gives the flavor that counts!
Look at the Bee Brand Extract bottle. Built like a pyramid—it won't tip! Has handy finger grips on sides—it won't slip! Has screw cap for easy opening and closing—it won't drip!

Tested and Approved by

GOOD HOUSEKEEPING   DELINEATOR
PARENTS' MAGAZINE   HOUSEHOLD SEARCHLIGHT

1936

McCormick employees worked two extra half days and contributed a full day's pay to the Community Fund in 1936. This was the predecessor to Charity Day, begun in 1941.

The McCormick Tea Museum opened in the Light Street building.

The former King of England abdicated the throne. The following year he married Wallis Warfield Simpson in France. Four years later, the Duke and Duchess of Windsor, as they were known thereafter, came to her native city of Baltimore.

Morning and afternoon rest periods for employees were established. Tea was served free.

Honey and spice make these snaps special.

¾ cup butter
1 cup sugar
¼ cup honey
1 egg
2 cups sifted flour
¼ teaspoon salt
2 teaspoons baking soda
1 teaspoon ground Cinnamon
1 teaspoon ground Cloves
1 teaspoon ground Ginger
¼ cup Cinnamon Sugar

Cream butter and sugar together. Add honey and egg; beat well. Sift flour, measure, and sift again with next 5 ingredients. Add to butter mixture and mix thoroughly. Roll into small balls and dip into cinnamon sugar or leave plain. Place 2 inches apart on greased baking sheet. Bake in 375°F. oven 10 to 12 minutes.

CAN DO AHEAD
FREEZES WELL

Makes 6 to 7 dozen cookies

1   17-ounce package pound cake mix
¼ cup Poppy Seed
½ teaspoon imitation Vanilla Butter & Nut Flavor
Glaze (recipe below)

Prepare pound cake, using amounts of milk and eggs called for in package directions. Stir in poppy seed and imitation vanilla butter & nut flavor. Bake following package directions. Cool 10 minutes in pan. Turn out on wire rack. Glaze while warm.

Makes one 9 x 5 x 3-inch loaf cake

Glaze: Mix 2 cups confectioners' sugar with 2 tablespoons hot water and ½ teaspoon imitation Vanilla Butter & Nut Flavor. Stir in ¼ teaspoon ground Cinnamon and dash of ground Mace. Spread over warm Poppy Seed Cake.

1937

The Tea House Tea trademark was introduced. New metal containers were developed for the spice line—one of the packaging changes that won seven national packaging awards for McCormick in the next two years.

The first issue of a new in-house magazine called *The Clipper* was issued.

The Company employed about 600 people.

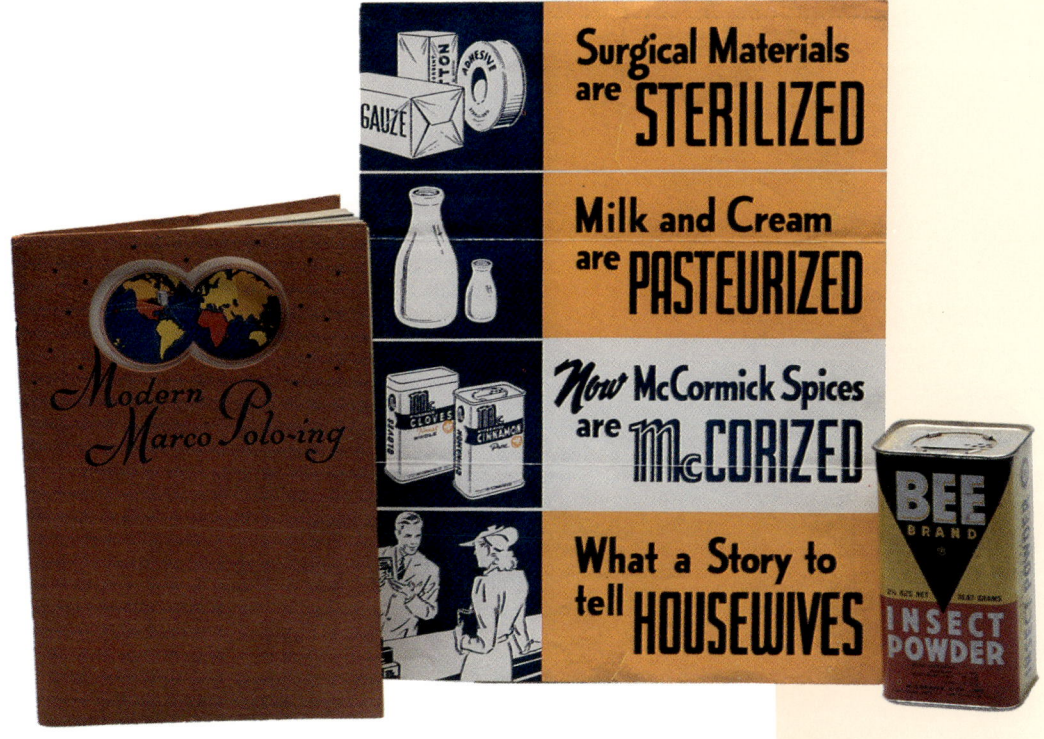

DEPRESSION CAKE

1938

The first spice fumigation process in the country was started. It was called ''McCorization'' or ''McCorized Products.''

C. P. McCormick's books—*Multiple Management* and *The McCormick System of Management*—went into print for the first time.

''Mc'' packaging logo introduced. The new logo was first used on lithographed tin canisters for tea bags and was extended to extract, spice, food color and condiment packages the following year.

So-named because it was developed during hard times when rich ingredients were unavailable.

2 cups flour
1 cup sugar
¼ cup unsweetened cocoa powder
1 teaspoon baking powder
½ teaspoon baking soda
1 teaspoon ground Cinnamon
½ teaspoon ground Cloves
½ teaspoon ground Nutmeg
1 cup mayonnaise
1 cup water
2 teaspoons pure Vanilla Extract
½ cup raisins
½ cup chopped walnuts
Glaze (recipe below)

Stir together first 8 ingredients. Set aside. Combine mayonnaise, water and vanilla. Add mayonnaise mixture to dry ingredients. Beat until blended, about 2 minutes. Fold in raisins and walnuts. Pour into greased and floured 9 x 9 x 2-inch baking pan. Bake in 350°F. oven 30 to 35 minutes or until cake tests done. Cool on wire rack 5 minutes. Remove cake from pan. Cool. Spread glaze over cake.

CAN DO AHEAD
MAKES A GREAT SNACKING CAKE

Makes one 9 x 9 x 2-inch cake

Glaze: Combine 1 cup confectioners' sugar, 2 tablespoons water and ½ teaspoon imitation Rum Extract. Mix well. Spread evenly over Depression Cake.

FREEZER TRAY ICE CREAM

Between 1930 and 1940, the electric refrigerator began to replace the old ice box. Freezer tray ice cream soon became a new and popular treat.

1   14-ounce can sweetened condensed milk
1 cup water
2 teaspoons pure Vanilla Extract
2 cups whipping cream

Combine first 3 ingredients. Mix well. Chill 15 minutes in freezer. Whip cream until thickened. Fold into chilled milk mixture. Pour into two ice cube freezing trays without dividers or one 8 x 8 x 2-inch glass dish. Freeze until mixture is slushy in texture, about 2½ to 3 hours. Turn into chilled bowl and beat until fluffy but not melted. Pour into freezer trays or glass dish. Freeze until solid.

EASY
MUST DO AHEAD

Makes 4½ cups

1939

Pioneering with Products and People, dedicated by C.P. to Willoughby McCormick, reviewed the Company's first 50 years.

The Company offered "Bru-o-lator" teapots to consumers for 75¢ and four tea cannister tops.

Seabiscuit defeated War Admiral in the "Race of the Century" at Pimlico.

World War II... The Atomic Age

In 1940, Franklin D. Roosevelt became the first President to win a third term of office. The country poised for war. In ''a day that will live in infamy,'' the Japanese struck Pearl Harbor, Hawaii, on Sunday, December 7, 1941. Congress declared war the next day.

The war years were full of shortages as Americans tried to make do. As a way to ration fairly, the government issued stamps for food and gasoline. Women took production jobs replacing men in factories, and ''Rosie the Riveter'' sang ''Praise the Lord and Pass the Ammunition'' along with the rest of the nation. Rita Hayworth, Betty Grable and Lana Turner were popular pin-ups. The big-band sounds of Tommy Dorsey and Harry James kept the mood of the public optimistic. ''Bobbie soxers'' swooned over Frank Sinatra and Bing Crosby records. Shows by Bob Hope entertained G.I.s at home and overseas. ''Kilroy was here,'' there and everywhere!

As Allied armies closed in on Germany in the spring of 1945, Roosevelt died suddenly. Vice President Harry S Truman, whose motto would become ''the buck stops here,'' succeeded him. Germany surrendered in May. In Japan, after other peace measures failed, President Truman ordered the newly developed atomic bomb dropped on Hiroshima and Nagasaki. The birth of the atomic age made war ''too horrible to contemplate.'' The worst war in history ended when Japan surrendered in 1945. The G.I. Bill of Rights established veterans' benefits.

In 1946, delegates from 51 nations met in London for the first General Assembly of the United Nations.

The G.I.s came home. Their new taste for Italian food caused sales of oregano to jump 400%. Shortages of automobiles and clothing eased. ''Zoot suits'' and flat pork-pie hats were in style. The public flocked to see such movies as *The Best Years of Our Lives* and hummed happy tunes: ''Zip-a-dee-doo-da,'' ''Doin' What Comes Naturally'' and ''Shoofly Pie.'' The Truman Doctrine gave aid to Greece and Turkey, and the Marshall Plan extended $12 billion to help finance the European recovery.

At home, inflation was a problem. New industries offered television, plastics, frozen foods, jet airplanes and automatic home appliances. *Annie Get Your Gun* was a hit on Broadway. Winston Churchill described Russia's ''Iron Curtain'' at a speech in Fulton, Missouri.

In 1948, Truman was reelected, fooling most of the nation's pollsters and many newspaper editors. A *Chicago Tribune* headline ''elected'' Dewey.

Spaghetti with Meatballs (pages 60–61)

1940

The first issue of a new in-house magazine, *The McCormick Family News*, was published.

McCormick Overseas Trading Corporation, later renamed the International Division, was formed to handle foreign operations.

The population of Baltimore increased from 850,000 to 940,000 during World War II.

Bee Brand Disinfectant for household use was introduced.

The Bethlehem Steel Company's shipyard in South Baltimore employed 47,000 at its peak and built 508 ships, including the first liberty ship freighter of the war.

The first Unsung Hero Award was presented. It was given by C.P. to "the unheralded high school athlete who contributed substantially to the success of the team."

The era of convenience foods began when many women were employed outside the home during World War II.

1 *1½-ounce package Spaghetti Sauce Mix*
1 *6-ounce can tomato paste*
2¼ cups water
1 tablespoon butter
½ teaspoon Italian Seasoning
½ teaspoon Instant Minced Onion
1 pound ground beef
1 teaspoon Seasoning Salt
¼ teaspoon ground Black Pepper
¼ teaspoon Instant Onion Powder
2 tablespoons vegetable oil
½ teaspoon Beef Flavor Base
¼ cup hot tap water
½ pound spaghetti

Combine first 6 ingredients in saucepan. Heat to a boil. Cover and simmer 20 minutes. Combine beef, seasoning salt, black pepper and onion powder. Mix well. Shape into 8 balls (1½ inches in diameter). Brown in hot oil. Dissolve beef flavor base in water. Pour over meatballs. Cover and simmer 20 minutes. Cook spaghetti, following package directions. Serve sauce over spaghetti. Top with meatballs.

EASY   *Makes 2½ cups sauce, 8 meatballs*

(see photo page 58)

MICROWAVE DIRECTIONS

Omit ingredients and reduce water as indicated. In a medium microwavable bowl, combine first 6 ingredients, reducing water to 1¾ cups (from 2¼ cups). Microcook, covered, on High 8 to 10 minutes, rotating and stirring once. Set aside. Combine beef, seasoning salt, black pepper and onion powder. Mix well. Shape in 1-inch meatballs. Omit oil, flavor base and hot tap water. Arrange meatballs in a microwavable 10-inch pie plate. Microcook, covered, on 50% power (Medium) 6 to 8 minutes, turning and rearranging meatballs once. Let stand 2 minutes. Drain excess liquid. Cook spaghetti, following package directions. Serve sauce over spaghetti. Top with meatballs.

QUICK AND EASY   *Makes 2 cups sauce, 20 to 22 meatballs*

LASAGNA

The popularity of Italian foods grew by leaps and bounds during the late forties.

1 pound ground beef
1   1½-ounce package Spaghetti Sauce Mix
1   6-ounce can tomato paste
1⅓ cups water
1 tablespoon butter
1 teaspoon Oregano Leaves
½ pound lasagna noodles
2 cups cottage cheese or ricotta cheese
½ pound mozzarella cheese slices

Brown ground beef in saucepan. Drain excess fat. Add next 5 ingredients. Mix well. Heat to a boil. Reduce heat, cover, and simmer 10 minutes. Cook noodles, following package directions. Rinse in cold water. Drain and separate. In buttered 11¾ x 7½ x 1¾-inch baking dish, make two layers of noodles, meat sauce, cottage cheese and slices of mozzarella cheese, in this order. Bake in 350°F. oven 25 minutes or until bubbly.

EASY
FREEZES WELL   *Makes 6 servings, 3½ x 4 inches each*

1942

The McCormick Glee Club was established with 20 members.

A potato dehydration plant was built in Maine at the request of the U.S. Army. The Company also pioneered in DDT, which saved thousands of lives from typhus and malaria. McCormick was the only company in the food industry to receive six wartime awards: four Army and Navy ''E''s and two Department of Agriculture ''A''s.

1943

A Profit Sharing Trust Agreement was established for employees.

On August 25, the Company was awarded an Army-Navy ''E'' flag for excellence in war production.

Baking Magic, an imitation vanilla extract, was offered during the war to consumers as a substitute for pure vanilla.

4 slices bread
1 1.25-ounce package Cheese Sauce Mix
1¼ cups milk
¼ teaspoon salt
¼ teaspoon ground Mustard
Dash Instant Minced Onion
Dash ground White Pepper
3 eggs, beaten
1 10-ounce package frozen broccoli spears
1 cup diced ham

Place bread in single layer on bottom of 8 x 8 x 2-inch baking dish. In saucepan, combine cheese sauce mix and next 5 ingredients. Cook, stirring constantly, until slightly thickened. Gradually add beaten eggs, stirring constantly. Cook 3 minutes over low heat. Cook broccoli until tender-crisp, about 5 minutes. Drain. Arrange spears evenly over bread. Top with ham. Pour sauce over entire mixture. Bake in 325°F. oven 20 minutes.

Makes 6 servings, 4 x 2½ inches each

SPICE CHIFFON CAKE

A twentieth-century invention, the first new cake in 100 years, substitutes oil for shortening, resulting in a light, moist cake.

2¼ cups sifted cake flour
1 tablespoon baking powder
1 teaspoon salt
1½ teaspoons Pumpkin Pie Spice
1½ cups sugar
½ cup vegetable oil
½ teaspoon pure Vanilla Extract
5 egg yolks
¾ cup cold water
1 cup (7 to 8) egg whites, at room temperature
½ teaspoon Cream of Tartar

Sift cake flour before measuring. Sift together first 4 ingredients and ½ cup of the sugar. Set aside. Beat together vegetable oil, vanilla, egg yolks and cold water. Gradually add dry ingredients. Mix at medium speed 2 minutes. Set aside. In large bowl, beat egg whites and cream of tartar until foamy. Gradually add remaining 1 cup sugar. Beat until stiff peaks form when beaters are lifted. Pour batter in thin stream over entire surface of beaten egg whites, gently cutting and folding in with rubber spatula. DO NOT STIR. Fold gently, bringing spatula across bottom of bowl, up the side and over. Turn bowl and continue until completely blended. Pour into an ungreased 10-inch tube pan. Bake in 325°F. oven 55 minutes. Increase oven temperature to 350°F. and bake 10 minutes longer. Invert immediately on funnel or bottle. Let cake stand until completely cool before removing from pan.

Makes one 10-inch tube cake

Note: You may substitute ¾ teaspoon ground Cinnamon and ¼ teaspoon each ground Nutmeg, Allspice and Cloves for Pumpkin Pie Spice.

A rich and velvety dark chocolate cake. The Fudge Frosting can be applied while the cake is still warm.

¾ cup butter
2¼ cups sugar
2 teaspoons pure Vanilla Extract
1 teaspoon ground Cinnamon
6 eggs
4   1-ounce squares unsweetened baking chocolate, melted
3 cups sifted cake flour
2 teaspoons baking soda
1 teaspoon salt
1½ cups ice water
Fudge Frosting (recipe opposite)

Cream together butter, sugar, vanilla and cinnamon until smooth and fluffy. Add eggs and beat until light and fluffy. Beat in melted chocolate. Sift cake flour before measuring. Sift together cake flour, baking soda and salt. Add ⅓ of the dry ingredients to the chocolate mixture. Stir in, using wire whisk. Add ½ of the ice water. Stir in. Repeat using ⅓ of the dry ingredients and the remaining ice water, then stir in remaining dry ingredients. Divide batter evenly among three greased, wax paper lined, 9-inch round layer cake pans. Bake in 350°F. oven 35 to 40 minutes. Do not over bake. Cool 10 minutes in pans. Remove from pans. Place one layer on serving plate. Spread with a small amount of Fudge Frosting. Add second layer and spread with frosting. Add top layer. Spread top and sides with Fudge Frosting.

Makes three 9-inch layers

Fudge Frosting: In stainless steel bowl over boiling water, combine two 12-ounce packages semi-sweet chocolate chips, one 14-ounce can sweetened condensed milk, ½ teaspoon ground Cinnamon and 1 teaspoon pure Vanilla Extract. Cover bowl with foil. Remove pan from heat. Let stand until chocolate is melted. Add ½ cup Kahlua (coffee liqueur) and stir until smooth and glossy.

Frosts one 3-layer cake, 9 inches in diameter

Notes: Cake can also be baked in one 13 x 9 x 3-inch pan. Bake in 350°F. oven 1 hour. Frost cake, using ½ recipe for Fudge Frosting.
May substitute raspberry preserves or chocolate pudding for Fudge Frosting between cake layers.

Rich, buttery, traditional shortbread, a wonderful accompaniment to afternoon tea.

1¼ cups butter
⅛ teaspoon ground Mace
⅛ teaspoon ground Nutmeg
¼ teaspoon Almond Extract
2½ cups sifted flour
¼ teaspoon salt
1 cup confectioners' sugar

Allow butter to soften at room temperature. Beat at low speed until consistency is even throughout. Beat in mace, nutmeg and almond extract. Gradually add flour, salt and sugar. Do not use electric mixer for this step. Mix thoroughly. Pack into 8-inch diameter, 1-inch deep shortbread mold. Press firmly and level the top. Bake in 250°F. oven 2½ hours. Cool 30 minutes in pan. Turn out on serving plate.

CAN DO AHEAD
FREEZES WELL

Makes 1 shortbread, 8 inches
in diameter and 1 inch thick

1948

Consolidated sales surpassed $25 million.

WBAL-TV began broadcasting in Baltimore.

1949

Stock split 4-for-1.

Multiple Management by C.P. McCormick was republished as *The Power of People.*

The Institutional Sales Board was established.

The first issue of a new in-house magazine, *Tea Time Tales*, was published.

Mace

Rock 'n' Roll

The Korean War broke out in June of 1950 when Russian-trained armies from North Korea invaded South Korea. Truman ordered U.S. forces to the aid of South Korea.

In 1952, popular war hero Dwight Eisenhower became President. He charted a moderate path, stressing teamwork over party politics. He promised to visit Korea and end the conflict. He did in 1953.

Casserole dishes and Sloppy Joe sandwiches were food favorites.

The first hydrogen bomb was exploded at Eniwetok atoll. The nation was stronger and richer than ever before, but problems of Communist influence and race relations took the spotlight. Eleven leaders of the U.S. Communist Party were convicted of spying. The McCarthy hearings on TV captured everyone's attention. In 1954, the Supreme Court ruled that public segregation was unconstitutional. The integration of schools triggered problems in many communities. Dr. Martin Luther King, Jr., gained national prominence by advocating "sit-ins" and passive resistance to segregation. Federal troops were called to permit black children to enter schools in Little Rock, Arkansas. The Civil Rights Act was passed.

Elvis Presley was the sensational singing success of the decade. His recordings of "Hound Dog" and "Heartbreak Hotel" broke all existing sales records. He became the hip-swinging, official symbol of Rock 'n' Roll. Film star Grace Kelly's marriage to Prince Rainier of Monaco was the romantic wedding of the fifties. With their win in 1953, the New York Yankees became the first team to win five consecutive World Series.

In 1958, the Baltimore Colts beat the New York Giants in overtime in the NFL championship game. It's been called the "greatest game ever played."

Dr. Jonas Salk developed a vaccine against polio. The Russians launched a satellite called *Sputnik*. Coeds came home from Eastern schools wearing Bermuda shorts, and the general public read the shocking true-to-life episodes of *Peyton Place*. *Auntie Mame* was another best-selling book, and the musical *My Fair Lady* broke all records on Broadway. Alaska and Hawaii were admitted as states.

Lobster with Vanilla Sauce (page 78)

1950

The census revealed that Baltimore had become the sixth largest city in the U.S.

Baltimore's Blaze Starr began showcasing her talents at the city's Two O'Clock Club.

Russell Baker (later a *New York Times* columnist) attended The Johns Hopkins University and began his journalism career as a Baltimore *Sun* police reporter.

A delicious new version of an old Maryland specialty. Best made with the backfin meat of the Blue Crab.

1 pound backfin crabmeat
1 cup dairy sour cream
1 cup mayonnaise
1 teaspoon Instant Minced Onion
¼ teaspoon Madras Curry Powder
½ teaspoon Dill Weed
½ teaspoon Bon Appétit
½ cup sliced almonds

Pick over crabmeat to remove cartilage. Combine sour cream with next 5 ingredients. Mix well. Add to crabmeat and mix thoroughly but lightly. Spoon into a shallow 1-quart casserole or quiche dish. Sprinkle sliced almonds over crab mixture. Bake in 350°F. oven 20 minutes. Keep hot for serving.

EASY   *Makes 3¾ cups*

Note: Can be made ahead except for cooking.

 MICROWAVE DIRECTIONS

Use same ingredients. Pick over crabmeat to remove cartilage. Combine sour cream with next 5 ingredients. Mix well. Add to crabmeat and mix thoroughly but lightly. Spoon into a microwavable 10-inch pie plate or quiche dish. Microcook, covered, on 50% power (Medium) 6 minutes, stirring and rotating twice. Sprinkle sliced almonds over crab mixture. Microcook, uncovered, on 25% power (Low) 3 minutes. Keep hot for serving.

QUICK AND EASY   *Makes 3¾ cups*

PISTACHIO-CHEESE DIP

1 8-ounce package cream cheese, softened
2 tablespoons crumbled blue cheese
½ cup half-and-half
1 tablespoon lemon juice
½ cup chopped salted pistachio nuts
½ teaspoon Instant Garlic Powder
1 teaspoon Bon Appétit

Blend together cream cheese and blue cheese. Gradually add half-and-half. Add remaining ingredients. Mix well. Chill thoroughly.

EASY
MUST DO AHEAD

Makes 1½ cups

1950

The Company's Bulk and Institutional Division added soup mixes, chicken flavor base and instant chocolate mix to the product line.

McCormick and Schilling products were distributed throughout the U.S. and exported to 44 countries. The slogan ''From All the World—Known the World Over'' was used for the first time.

Friendship International Airport, later renamed Baltimore-Washington International Airport, was dedicated by President Harry Truman, after a construction cost of $15 million.

TANGY COLESLAW

The food processor speeds slaw cutting.

6 tablespoons dairy sour cream
6 tablespoons mayonnaise
1 tablespoon Instant Minced Onion
2 teaspoons Parsley Flakes
2 tablespoons sugar
1¼ teaspoons Seasoning Salt
¼ teaspoon Celery Seed
½ teaspoon ground Mustard
1 tablespoon vinegar
¼ teaspoon ground Black Pepper
6 cups shredded green cabbage

Combine all ingredients except cabbage. Mix well. Let stand 10 minutes. Add cabbage to dressing. Toss well. Chill thoroughly before serving.

EASY
MUST DO AHEAD

Makes 5 cups

1951

McCormick Western Hemisphere Corporation was organized to conduct business in Central and South America.

The Eisenhower Award was presented by McCormick for excellence in the fields of psychology and leadership: the first of five annual service academy awards.

New spice containers with improved spoon-sift openings and new sliding closures were introduced.

A favorite in the fifties.

> 2   9-ounce packages frozen
> French-cut green beans
> 1   10¾-ounce can condensed cream of mushroom soup
> ¼ cup milk
> ¼ teaspoon Seasoning Salt
> ⅛ teaspoon ground Black Pepper
> 1 tablespoon dry sherry
> 2 tablespoons chopped pimiento, drained
> 1 2.8-ounce can French-fried onions

Cook green beans, following package directions. Drain. In 1½-quart casserole, combine green beans and next 6 ingredients. Add ½ of the onions. Mix well. Bake in 350°F. oven, uncovered, 20 minutes. Top with remaining onions. Bake 5 minutes longer.

QUICK AND EASY   *Makes 3½ cups*

Note: May substitute 3 cups fresh cut green beans, cooked, or two 16-ounce cans green beans, drained, for frozen green beans.

  MICROWAVE DIRECTIONS

Use same ingredients, reducing milk as indicated. Place frozen green beans, icy side up, in 2-quart microwavable casserole. Microcook, covered, on High 9 to 11 minutes, stirring and rotating twice. Drain. Combine green beans with next 6 ingredients, reducing milk to 2 tablespoons (from ¼ cup). Add ½ of the onions. Mix well. Top with remaining onions. Microcook, uncovered, on High 6 to 7 minutes. Remove from oven and let stand 5 minutes.

Makes 3½ cups

HERBED CORN-ON-THE-COB

This corn is a special treat, whether prepared outdoors on the grill or served, year-round, piping hot from the microwave.

6 ears of corn, in husks
½ cup butter, softened
1 teaspoon Instant Minced Onion
½ teaspoon Basil Leaves
½ teaspoon Marjoram Leaves
¼ teaspoon Bon Appétit
¼ teaspoon Seasoning Salt
½ teaspoon Paprika
Dash ground Red Pepper

Loosen husks of corn enough to remove silk. Soak in cold water 30 minutes or longer. When ready to roast, drain well. Combine remaining ingredients and spread generously over corn. Rewrap husks, then wrap in aluminum foil. Place on grill about 5 inches from coals. Cook 25 minutes, turning several times. Remove foil and husks. Serve hot.

EASY
OUTDOOR COOKING
Makes 6 ears of corn

MICROWAVE DIRECTIONS

Use same ingredients, except use 4 ears frozen corn, and change amounts as indicated. In a microwavable 2-cup measuring cup, microcook ¼ cup butter (reduced from ½ cup), uncovered, on 50% power (Medium) 1 minute. Add next 7 ingredients. Microcook, uncovered, on 25% power (Low) 2 minutes. Set aside. Rinse frost, if any, from frozen corn. Drain. Place corn in a shallow 1½-quart microwavable casserole. Microcook, covered, on High 10 to 12 minutes, turning corn and rotating once. Let stand 5 minutes. Drain. Pour butter mixture over corn. Turn ears to coat evenly. Microcook, covered, on 25% power (Low) 2 minutes, turning corn and rotating once. Serve hot.

QUICK AND EASY
Makes 4 ears of corn

1952

The Chesapeake Bay Bridge was dedicated.

A 20% stock dividend was declared.

The Company celebrated C. P.'s 20th anniversary as President of McCormick with a dinner at the Belvedere Hotel.

SICILIAN PIZZA

1953

Carroll Rosenbloom bought the Dallas, Texas, football franchise and re-created the Baltimore Colts. They finished the season winning one out of 12 games.

A thick, soft-crust pizza loaded with goodies.

1   *16-ounce package hot roll mix*
1   *6-ounce can tomato paste*
1½ cups water
½ teaspoon Basil Leaves
½ teaspoon Oregano Leaves
¼ teaspoon cracked Black Pepper

Toppings:

Italian Sausage, mild or hot, sliced and cooked
Mushrooms, sliced
Green pepper, seeded and chopped
Red pepper, seeded and chopped
Onion, peeled and chopped
Bacon, cooked and crumbled
Mozzarella cheese, shredded

Prepare hot roll mix, following package directions. Put dough in a lightly oiled 15 x 11 x 1-inch jelly roll pan. Press dough to line bottom and sides of pan. In saucepan, combine tomato paste with next 4 ingredients. Heat to a boil, reduce heat, and simmer 30 minutes. Pour over crust, spreading to coat evenly. Sprinkle your choice of toppings over the sauce. Top with shredded cheese. Bake in 375°F. oven 30 minutes.

Makes one 15 x 11-inch pizza

½ pound thin veal cutlets
½ pound veal sweetbreads
½ cup butter
1 tablespoon flour
½ cup malt vinegar
⅔ cup water
¼ teaspoon ground Mustard
¼ teaspoon Paprika
⅛ teaspoon Thyme Leaves
⅛ teaspoon Tarragon Leaves
¼ teaspoon ground Black Pepper
¼ teaspoon Instant Minced Onion
Salad greens

Cut veal in small pieces, about 2 x 2 x ¼ inches. Parboil sweetbreads. Cool. Remove membrane and cut meat in small pieces, about 2 x 2 x ½ inches. Sauté veal and sweetbreads in butter until lightly browned. Remove meat and keep warm. Sprinkle flour over butter in skillet. Stir and cook over low heat 1 minute. Add vinegar, water and next 6 ingredients. Cook, stirring and scraping pan, 1 minute. Pour into heatproof bowl and keep warm. Arrange four plates of salad greens. Place meat, alternating slices of veal and sweetbreads, over center of greens. Pour ¼ cup of sauce over meat. Serve immediately.

Makes 4 individual salads
Sauce makes 1 cup

½ cup flour
1 teaspoon salt
½ teaspoon ground Black Pepper
½ teaspoon Instant Garlic Powder
½ teaspoon ground Ginger
12 broiler/fryer chicken drumsticks
½ cup butter
½ cup hot water
½ teaspoon Chicken Flavor Base
½ teaspoon Lemon & Pepper Seasoning Salt
½ teaspoon Sage Leaves
1 cup light cream

In plastic bag, mix flour, salt, pepper, garlic powder and ginger. Add drumsticks, a few at a time, and shake to coat well. Repeat until all drumsticks are coated with seasoned flour. Melt butter in large heavy skillet. Brown drumsticks on all sides. Use low heat to brown the chicken slowly and evenly. Remove drumsticks to shallow baking pan. Pour butter from skillet over chicken, leaving the brown drippings in the skillet. Bake drumsticks in 350°F. oven 50 minutes. Measure the water and add chicken flavor base, lemon & pepper seasoning salt and sage. Pour into skillet. Heat to a boil and stir to dissolve the drippings. Stir in cream. Heat to a boil. Reduce heat and simmer until slightly thickened. Pour over drumsticks on serving platter.

Makes 12 drumsticks, 1⅓ cups gravy

1955

The Company was identified as "The House of Flavor."

A birchwood spice rack was offered to consumers for $3 as a promotion for the Company's vanilla.

Whole sesame seed was added to the product line.

Generous use of paprika gives this special chicken a smooth and mellow flavor.

> 1 *3-pound broiler/fryer chicken, cut in pieces*
> *½ cup flour*
> *1 teaspoon Seasoning Salt*
> *½ teaspoon ground Thyme*
> *¼ teaspoon coarse grind Black Pepper*
> *½ cup shortening*
> *2 tablespoons Paprika*
> *½ teaspoon Garlic Salt*
> *2 cups hot water*
> *2 medium onions*
> *2 tablespoons flour*
> *½ cup milk*

Wash chicken; pat dry. Combine flour, seasoning salt, thyme and pepper. Coat chicken pieces with flour mixture and fry in hot shortening until lightly browned on all sides. Combine paprika and garlic salt and sprinkle over chicken. Add hot water and simmer 30 minutes. Slice onions and separate into rings. Place on top of chicken and simmer 30 minutes longer. Remove chicken to serving platter and pile onions on top. Blend together flour and milk; add to liquid in pan. Cook until thickened; pour over chicken.

Makes 6 pieces chicken

BARBECUED COUNTRY RIBS

Spicy country ribs, cooked outdoors.

½ cup red wine vinegar
¼ cup salad oil
½ cup tomato sauce
1 tablespoon Chili Powder
2 teaspoons Seasoning Salt
2 teaspoons Salad Supreme®
1 teaspoon Celery Seed
1 teaspoon Lemon & Pepper Seasoning Salt
½ teaspoon ground Cumin
5 pounds country-style pork spareribs

Combine all ingredients except spareribs and mix well. Cut spareribs in large serving pieces and place in plastic bag. Add the oil-vinegar mixture and close bag. Chill 2 hours or longer, turning the bag occasionally so marinade covers the meat. When ready to cook, drain, saving the marinade. Grill slowly about 8 inches from coals, 40 minutes or until well done, turning and basting frequently (about every 5 to 8 minutes) with marinade.

EASY
OUTDOOR COOKING

Makes 5 pounds ribs, approximately 8 servings

1955

The Ben-Hur name was dropped from the logo and changed to McCormick/Schilling.

John Curlett became the Company's third President. C. P. McCormick remained Chairman of the Board.

C. P. was named Chairman of the Civic Center Commission in Baltimore.

Delightful variation on the classic lobster with butter.

1 cup butter
½ teaspoon lemon juice
¼ teaspoon pure Vanilla Extract
Hot steamed lobsters (3 to 4)

Melt butter in small saucepan. Remove from heat. Cool slightly. Carefully pour off the clear portion into a small mixing bowl. Add lemon juice and vanilla. Mix well. Serve sauce hot with steamed lobster.

QUICK AND EASY   *Makes ¾ cup*

(see photo page 66)

CARAWAY-CHEESE BATTER BREAD

1 cup milk
½ cup butter
¼ cup water
⅓ cup sugar
2 teaspoons salt
2 ¼-ounce packages active dry yeast
4 cups sifted flour
3 eggs
1 tablespoon Caraway Seed
1 teaspoon Instant Minced Onion
⅔ cup grated Cheddar cheese

Heat milk, butter and water until warm (120°F.). Blend sugar, salt, yeast and 1⅓ cups of the flour in large mixing bowl. Gradually stir warm liquid into flour mixture. Beat with electric mixer at medium speed 2 minutes. Gradually add eggs and ⅔ cup of the flour. Beat at high speed 2 minutes. Add remaining flour and remaining 3 ingredients. Mix at low speed just until blended. Do not overmix. Batter will be thick but not stiff. Cover and let rise in warm, draft-free place (about 85°F.) until double in bulk (about 75 minutes). Beat dough down with spatula and turn into greased and floured 10-inch bundt pan. Cover and let rise in a warm, draft-free place until double in bulk (about 30 minutes). Bake in 350°F. oven 40 to 50 minutes or until golden brown on top. Run knife around center and outer edges of bread and turn out on wire rack to cool.

CAN DO AHEAD   *Makes one 10-inch round loaf*

1956

Country singer and songwriter Johnny Cash became an overnight success with the release of "I Walk the Line."

On the "Ed Sullivan Show," Elvis Presley was shown only from the waist up. CBS censored the singer's hips so his wild gyrations wouldn't offend viewers.

1957

The Company celebrated the 25th anniversary of Multiple Management. New products included Fun Brand Soda Mix, Fluffy Instant Mashed Potatoes and Russet Potato Nuggets.

Makes a rich, moist brownie with a creamy Chocolate-Cinnamon Fudge Frosting.

½ cup butter
3 1-ounce squares unsweetened chocolate
1½ cups sugar
3 eggs
¼ teaspoon salt
1 teaspoon pure Vanilla Extract
1 cup sifted flour
¾ cup coarsely chopped walnuts
Chocolate-Cinnamon Fudge Frosting (recipe below)

In top of double boiler over hot water, melt butter and chocolate. Remove from heat. Combine chocolate mixture and sugar. Add eggs, one at a time, beating well after each addition. Blend in remaining ingredients except frosting. Mix well. Pour into a greased and floured 9 x 9 x 2-inch baking pan. Bake in 350°F. oven 20 to 25 minutes. Cool. Frost with Chocolate-Cinnamon Fudge Frosting.

Makes twelve 2¼ x 2¼-inch brownies

Chocolate-Cinnamon Fudge Frosting: In top of double boiler over hot water, melt two 1-ounce squares semi-sweet chocolate and ¼ cup butter. Remove from heat. Combine chocolate mixture with 1 teaspoon pure Vanilla Extract, ⅛ teaspoon ground Cinnamon and 1 cup sifted confectioners' sugar. Spread evenly over brownies. Garnish brownies with additional chopped walnuts, if desired.

Makes ¾ cup frosting

APPLE DUMPLINGS
WITH SPICED SYRUP

Fragrant spices make these dumplings superb.

6 medium baking apples, peeled and cored
1 tablespoon lemon juice
1 cup sugar
1 cup water
½ teaspoon ground Cinnamon
¼ teaspoon ground Nutmeg
⅛ teaspoon ground Cloves
Dash ground Mace
3 cups flour
1 cup whole wheat flour
½ teaspoon ground Cinnamon
4 teaspoons baking powder
1 teaspoon salt
½ cup softened butter
1¼ cups milk
4 tablespoons brown sugar
1 tablespoon butter
Dash ground Cinnamon
Dash ground Nutmeg

Put apples in a bowl of water with lemon juice. In saucepan, combine sugar with next 5 ingredients. Heat to boiling, reduce heat, and simmer 10 minutes. Set aside. In mixing bowl, blend both flours with next 3 ingredients. Cut butter into flour until mixture resembles coarse meal. Add ¾ cup of the milk and mix well, adding more milk as needed to make dough soft but not sticky. Knead on lightly floured board, about 15 seconds. Divide dough in half. Roll each piece into a rectangle 21 x 7 inches. Cut each rectangle in three 7 x 7-inch squares. Place one apple on each square. In the cavity of each apple, put 2 teaspoons brown sugar, ½ teaspoon butter and dash each of cinnamon and nutmeg. Lift edges of dough to meet over the top of each apple. Press seams together. Trim excess dough, if desired, and cut out 6 leaf shapes. Inscribe veins in each leaf. Moisten one end with water and press gently to attach at the top of each dumpling. Place dumplings in buttered baking pan. Pour the spiced syrup over dumplings. Bake in 350°F. oven 50 to 55 minutes, basting with syrup every 15 minutes. Serve warm.

Makes 6 apple dumplings

1957

McCormick de Venezuela, C.A., was formed as another joint venture.

The Baltimore Harbor Tunnel opened.

1958

The Baltimore Colts won their first NFL title as the Colts beat New York 23-17 in overtime.

A foil-packaged line was introduced, the first step in a convenience food line of fast and flavorful products for homemakers.

Clamato Juice—a combination of clam juice, tomato products and spices—was added to the product line.

C. P. was named ''Man of the Year'' by the National Conference of Christians and Jews.

Ice cream baked in a hot oven—how does it work?

Cake:

1 cup sifted cake flour
2 tablespoons confectioners' sugar
⅛ teaspoon salt
¼ teaspoon ground Ginger
¼ teaspoon ground Cinnamon
⅛ teaspoon ground Nutmeg
6 egg yolks
2 tablespoons melted butter
½ cup sugar
1 tablespoon honey
½ teaspoon pure Vanilla Extract

Ice Cream:

1 quart vanilla ice cream
1 pint strawberry ice cream
1 pint orange sherbet

Meringue:

6 egg whites
1½ cups sugar
1 teaspoon pure Vanilla Extract
¼ teaspoon Orange Extract

Cake: Grease one 10-inch round or 9-inch square cake pan. Dust with flour and line bottom with wax paper. Sift flour with confectioners' sugar, salt, ginger, cinnamon and nutmeg. Beat egg yolks until pale yellow. Add butter, sugar, honey and vanilla. Beat until sugar is completely dissolved. Fold in dry ingredients. Pour into prepared pan and bake in 350°F. oven 25 minutes. Cool on wire rack 10 minutes. Loosen edge and turn out of pan. Peel off wax paper. Cool. Invert on ovenproof serving dish or board.

Ice Cream: Use a shallow 2-quart bowl to mold ice cream. Cut the vanilla ice cream in 1-inch thick slices, line bowl and smooth surface to an even thickness. Make a layer of strawberry ice cream inside the vanilla. Fill center with orange sherbet. Cover with plastic wrap and freeze until firm. Unmold on the cake. Freeze cake and ice cream.

Meringue: Beat egg whites until foamy. Gradually add sugar while beating at high speed. Add extracts. Beat at high speed until stiff peaks form when beaters are lifted. Working quickly, spread meringue over ice cream and cake, covering evenly and completely. Be sure meringue is sealed to cake all around edges. (Baked Alaska can be frozen at this stage.) Just before serving, bake in preheated 450°F. oven 3 to 5 minutes, only until meringue tips begin to brown. Serve immediately.

Makes 1 Baked Alaska, 10-inch round or 9-inch square

LEMON GINGER ICE

Refreshing between courses or use as a light dessert.

2 cups water
1 cup sugar
1 cup lemon juice
1 drop Yellow Food Color
1 drop Anise Extract
1 tablespoon plus 1 teaspoon
minced Crystallized Ginger

In 2-quart saucepan, heat first 2 ingredients to a boil over medium heat. Stir only until sugar dissolves. Cook mixture 5 minutes. Remove pan from heat. Cool to room temperature. Stir in remaining ingredients. Pour mixture into an ice cube tray without divider. Freeze 4 hours, stirring every 30 minutes, scraping particles from around edges of tray into the middle.

EASY
MUST DO AHEAD

Makes 3 cups

1959

The Company acquired Gorman Eckert and Company, Ltd., a Canadian spice and extract company founded in 1883.

McCormick, S.A., a wholly owned subsidiary, was founded in Zurich, Switzerland, to market spices, extracts and other food products.

McCormick first presented the Vandenburg Award "to honor the outstanding cadet in airmanship studies at the United States Air Force Academy."

Space...
A New Frontier

In 1960, 43-year-old John F. Kennedy was elected the 35th President . . . the youngest ever to hold the office and the first Roman Catholic. A rock group from Liverpool, England, called The Beatles created the musical style of the era.

The Peace Corps was established. Problems with the spread of Communism persisted. Cuban rebels, supported by the U.S., failed in an attempt to overthrow Fidel Castro, and American prestige suffered at the "Bay of Pigs." The Kennedy administration was more successful in forcing the Russians to dismantle their missiles in Cuba.

High unemployment, inflation and an economic slow-down continued to trouble the nation. Racial tensions increased. Riots began in cities across the country.

Ralph Nader and other consumer activists challenged the entire range of buyer/seller relationships by demanding "social responsibility" for products. Belgian waffles were introduced at the World's Fair in New York City and have been popular ever since.

The U.S. space program gained momentum and success in the early Sixties. Astronauts Glenn, Shepard, Grissom and Carpenter circled the earth. In 1966, Edwin Aldrin stepped out of the spacecraft *Gemini 12* for a 129-minute walk in space televised in color across the U.S. In July 1969, Americans took the first steps on the surface of the moon.

First Lady Jacqueline Kennedy set the style in food and fashions. The sophisticated style and political and social vitality of the Kennedys made the tragedy of the President's assassination in Dallas in 1963 even more difficult for the nation to accept. Later, mini skirts, Texas barbecues and a dance called the "Twist" took over the scene.

The days of "Camelot" ended as Lyndon B. Johnson took over as President. The new President from Texas inherited an unpopular and escalating war in Vietnam and tried to solve the nation's social problems by establishing a "Great Society." Demonstrations against the Vietnam War began to grow in numbers and size, and civil rights riots continued to plague major cities.

Dr. Martin Luther King, Jr., and Senator Robert F. Kennedy were assassinated.

Republican Richard Nixon was elected President after Lyndon Johnson announced he would not run again. The Baltimore Orioles won their first World Series by sweeping the L.A. Dodgers in four straight games in 1966.

MICKEY MOUSE celebrated his 40th birthday. At the movies, audiences saw *Mary Poppins*, *Dr. Zhivago* and the James Bond thriller *Goldfinger*. Best sellers were Truman Capote's *In Cold Blood*, Jacqueline Susann's *Valley of the Dolls* and Ira Levin's *Rosemary's Baby*.

Top musicals were *The Sound of Music*, *Fiddler on the Roof*, *Hello Dolly* and *Hair*. The Woodstock Music Art Fair near Bethel, New York, attracted some 300,000 enthusiasts.

Australian Pavlova (page 96)

1960

The McCormick Division was established and organized as a separate operating unit.

The new Gourmet line of spices, herbs and spice blends was introduced nationally after a trial release in 1959. Public response to the new line exceeded expectations.

Maryland's State House, the oldest in continuous use, was designated a National Historic Landmark.

2 8-ounce packages cream cheese
1 teaspoon Fennel Seed
¼ teaspoon Bon Appétit
⅛ teaspoon ground Savory
⅛ teaspoon Instant Garlic Powder
⅛ teaspoon Instant Onion Powder
¼ teaspoon Basil Leaves
Whole almonds, with skins
Fresh chives
Fresh parsley

Allow cream cheese to soften at room temperature. Using an electric mixer, beat together cream cheese and next 6 ingredients. Mix well. Refrigerate mixture 4 hours or overnight. Mold into pineapple shape with hands. To cover cheese with almonds, start at bottom and work up in even rows. Push almonds into cheese mixture, pointed end down, overlapping in a shingled manner. Continue until cheese is covered with almonds, leaving a small space in top center. Poke small holes in top of ''pineapple'' and place tops of fresh chives into cheese. Place small sprigs of parsley around base of chives. Serve at room temperature.

MUST DO AHEAD   *Makes 1 cup cheese spread*

マコーミック
マスタード（西洋がらし）
爽やかな香り、マイルドな味の高級西洋がらしです。どんなお料理にもよく合いますが、とくに肉や魚のお料理に好適です。必要なだけをぬるま湯で溶き、5分間ほどおいてからお使いください。

ステーキ、ハンバーグ、焼きとり、バーベキュー、中華料理、えび・かに料理、魚料理、コロッケ、ホットドッグ、サンドイッチ、サラダドレッシング、ポテト、ロールキャベツ、漬物、納豆など。
マイルドな風味はフレンチマスタード用としても最適です。

製造元　ライオン曲磨（株）食品部Ｔ
発売元　ライオン食品株式会社
　　　　東京都墨田区本所1丁目3番
提　携　McCORMICK & CO., INC.
　　　　Baltimore, Maryland, U.S.A.

6 medium-size sweet potatoes (2½ x 5 inches)
¼ cup butter
1 tablespoon Instant Minced Onion
1 teaspoon Bon Appétit
¼ teaspoon ground Ginger
¼ teaspoon ground White Pepper
Dash ground Allspice
¼ cup Imitation Bacon Chips

Bake sweet potatoes in 375°F. oven 1 hour or until well cooked. Cut skin off the tops of potatoes. Scoop out flesh, leaving a thin layer all around to support the skins in 4 of the shells. Beat potato with butter and next 5 ingredients. Beat until smooth. Stir in bacon chips. Spoon into 4 of the potato shells. Bake in 350°F. oven 20 minutes. Sprinkle with additional bacon chips, if desired.

Makes 4 servings, 1 stuffed potato each

 MICROWAVE DIRECTIONS

Use same ingredients. Prick sweet potatoes over entire surface, using tines of a fork. Place in a circular pattern on the microwave oven floor. Microcook, uncovered, on High 16 to 18 minutes, rotating potatoes every 4 minutes. Let stand 8 minutes. Cut skin off the tops of potatoes. Scoop out flesh, leaving a thin layer all around to support the skins in 4 of the shells. Beat potato with butter and next 5 ingredients. Beat until smooth. Stir in bacon chips. Spoon into 4 of the potato shells. Arrange stuffed potatoes in a microwavable 10-inch pie plate. Microcook, uncovered, on 50% power (Medium) 4 to 6 minutes or until heated through. Sprinkle with more bacon chips, if desired.

Makes 4 servings, 1 stuffed potato each

1961

The Company acquired Gilroy Foods, Inc., a California-based producer of dehydrated onions and garlic. Gilroy sold its products to manufacturers and food processors nationally under the Golden West label.

McCormick Foods (U.K.) Limited was established in London.

The Company's consolidated sales topped $50 million.

La Bizkayna, S.A., of Panama City was licensed to produce McCormick salad products and mustards and to distribute imported McCormick products in Panama, Costa Rica and Nicaragua.

In Sweden, the spice firm of Kockens Aktiebolag was licensed to manufacture, package, sell and distribute the McCormick Gourmet line of spices in Scandinavia.

Yuri A. Gagarin was the first Russian in space, Alan B. Shepard, Jr., the first American.

1962

One Charles Center opened for occupancy—the first step in the revitalization of a new downtown Baltimore.

The Company established an International Division.

Authorized Common Stock increased to 200,000, Non-Voting to 600,000. Stock split 2-for-1.

Baker Extract Co. of Springfield, Massachusetts, was purchased by McCormick.

½ cup butter, cut in pieces
2 teaspoons Turmeric
1 teaspoon ground Cumin
½ teaspoon Instant Garlic Powder
⅛ teaspoon ground Nutmeg
¼ teaspoon ground Mustard
½ teaspoon ground White Pepper
½ teaspoon Instant Onion Powder
⅛ teaspoon ground Red Pepper
½ teaspoon ground Ginger
¼ teaspoon Thyme Leaves
1 Bay Leaf
2 tablespoons flour
2 teaspoons Chicken Flavor Base
3 tablespoons tomato paste
1¼ cups water
3 cups steamed vegetables (see below)

Melt butter. Stir in next 12 ingredients. Cook over low heat 5 minutes. Add chicken flavor base and tomato paste. Mix well. Gradually add water, stirring constantly until sauce thickens. Remove bay leaf. Serve over one or a combination of: steamed broccoli, cauliflower, carrots and zucchini.

Makes 1¾ cups sauce

Ginger

MICROWAVE DIRECTIONS

Use same ingredients, reducing water as indicated. Place butter pieces in medium microwavable bowl. Microcook, uncovered, on 50% power (Medium) 2 minutes. Blend in next 12 ingredients until smooth. Microcook, uncovered, on 25% power (Low) 4 to 5 minutes, stirring twice. Dissolve chicken flavor base and tomato paste in water, reducing water to ¾ cup (from 1¼ cups). Mix well, using wire whisk. Gradually add liquids to butter mixture, stirring until well blended. Microcook, uncovered, on 50% power (Medium) 3 to 4 minutes, rotating and stirring after every minute. Remove bay leaf. Serve over one or a combination of: steamed broccoli, cauliflower, carrots and zucchini.

Makes 1¼ cups sauce

1962

The French firm of Etablissements Maurice Daniel of Marseilles, France, was licensed to manufacture, package, sell and distribute the Gourmet line throughout France.

McCormick added a new dimension with its holdings in Maryland Properties, Inc., a real estate company established to design, build and manage Greater Baltimore Industrial Park, a 435-acre tract of land in Baltimore County subsequently named Hunt Valley Business Community. (In 1973, Maryland Properties became a wholly owned unconsolidated subsidiary; in 1979, it was renamed McCormick Properties, Inc.)

1963

The plastic duo-flip top for spice tins was introduced, the first of its type in the industry.

An Industrial Products Division was created to produce encapsulated flavors, soluble seasonings and custom flavoring blends for food processors.

McCormick spices, tea, coffee and potatoes accompanied the first American expedition to climb Mt. Everest.

John Glenn became the first American to orbit the earth.

Martin Luther King, Jr., stood in front of the Lincoln Memorial to give his famous speech, ''I have a dream.''

Good hot, or cold for picnics.

12 pieces broiler/fryer chicken
2 eggs
¼ cup water
¾ cup flour
½ teaspoon Turmeric
1 teaspoon salt
½ teaspoon Instant Onion Powder
¼ teaspoon ground White Pepper
½ cup Sesame Seed, lightly toasted
Oil for frying

Wash and dry chicken pieces. Beat eggs with water. Combine flour with next 5 ingredients. Mix well. Roll chicken in flour mixture, dip in egg and roll in flour mixture again. Fry in hot oil (350°F.) until well browned, 30 to 35 minutes. Drain on paper towels.

CAN DO AHEAD   *Makes 12 pieces fried chicken*

Note: To toast sesame seed, spread in shallow baking pan and heat in 350°F. oven 10 minutes or until lightly browned.

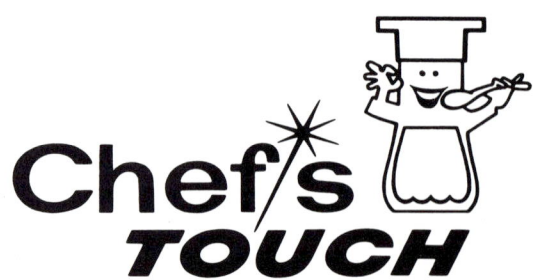

SUPRÊMES DE VOLAILLE À L'ÉCOSSAISE

¼ cup butter
⅓ cup finely diced carrots
⅓ cup finely diced green pepper
⅓ cup finely diced celery
2 tablespoons Instant Minced Onion
¼ teaspoon Marjoram Leaves
¼ teaspoon Basil Leaves
¼ teaspoon Thyme Leaves
1 tablespoon Parsley Flakes
¼ teaspoon ground White Pepper
8 half chicken breasts, boneless, skinless
1 teaspoon Chicken Flavor Base
1 cup hot water
1 cup light cream
¼ cup dry vermouth

Melt butter in large skillet. Add next 9 ingredients. Cook over low heat 10 minutes. Lay chicken breasts over vegetables. Cook 5 minutes on each side. Remove chicken (leave vegetables in skillet) to hot platter and place in warm oven. Add remaining ingredients to skillet. Stir and heat to boiling. Boil, stirring frequently, until sauce has thickened slightly. Pour over chicken. If desired, garnish chicken with small green peas and sautéed cherry tomatoes.

Makes 8 servings, ½ chicken breast each

1964

The Company celebrated its 75th anniversary. McCormick consisted of 24 operating division and subsidiary corporations selling products in 56 countries throughout the world.

Spices of the World Cookbook, published by McGraw-Hill, went on sale in leading book and department stores.

McCormick de Venezuela, C.A., became a wholly owned subsidiary of McCormick.

McCormick GmbH, a wholly owned subsidiary, was established in West Germany to oversee the production, distribution and sale of McCormick products throughout most of the European Common Market.

Topless bathing suits for women brought gasps and stares from Americans.

VEAL MARSALA

1965

Chef's Touch, a line of ready-mixed blends of spices, herbs and flavors, was introduced.

Television viewers were treated to the first live overseas television broadcasts via satellite on May 2.

¼ cup butter
2 cups sliced mushrooms
1½ pounds veal cutlets, cut ¼ inch thick
2 slices bacon, chopped
¼ cup flour
½ teaspoon Instant Garlic Powder
¼ teaspoon ground Black Pepper
½ teaspoon Seasoning Salt
¼ cup cold water
1 teaspoon cornstarch
½ cup dry Marsala wine
¼ teaspoon Instant Onion Powder
½ teaspoon Marjoram Leaves
¼ teaspoon Basil Leaves
¼ teaspoon Bon Appétit

In skillet, melt 1 tablespoon of the butter. Sauté mushrooms in hot butter. Remove from skillet; set aside. Cut veal into 12 serving-size pieces. In skillet, fry bacon over low heat until cooked but not crisp. Add 2 tablespoons of the butter to skillet. Combine flour, garlic powder, black pepper and seasoning salt. Dust veal with flour mixture and sauté, a few pieces at a time, over medium heat 2 minutes on each side. Add the remaining 1 tablespoon butter to skillet when needed. Place veal on serving platter. Keep warm. Slowly stir water into cornstarch. Add wine and remaining ingredients. Pour liquid into skillet along with mushrooms. Cook, stirring, over low heat until mixture begins to boil. Pour over veal.

Makes 6 servings, 2 pieces each

Note: May use boneless, skinless chicken breasts, pounded to ¼-inch thickness, in place of veal cutlets.

LAMB CHOPS WITH
HORSERADISH-PECAN SAUCE

6 slices bacon
6 boneless lamb loin chops, cut 1½ inches thick
1 tablespoon olive oil
1 tablespoon soy sauce
1 tablespoon lemon juice
⅛ teaspoon Instant Garlic Powder
⅛ teaspoon Instant Onion Powder
Horseradish-Pecan Sauce (recipe below)

Cook bacon over low heat until cooked but not crisp. Shape lamb chops into rounds. Wrap each chop with 1 piece bacon. Secure with wooden toothpick. Place lamb chops on broiler pan. Combine next 5 ingredients. Brush chops with mixture. Broil 4 inches from heat 10 minutes or until desired doneness. Turn chops once and brush occasionally during cooktime. Serve with Horseradish-Pecan Sauce. Garnish with fresh mint, if desired.

Makes 6 lamb chops

Horseradish-Pecan Sauce: Combine 1 tablespoon olive oil and 1 tablespoon flour in small saucepan. Add ⅛ teaspoon ground White Pepper, 1 teaspoon Bon Appétit and ⅛ teaspoon Instant Minced Garlic. Heat until bubbly. Gradually add 1 cup half-and-half, stirring constantly. Add 1 tablespoon prepared horseradish and ¼ cup chopped pecans. Cook over medium heat, stirring constantly, until mixture thickens.

Makes 1 cup sauce

1966

Salad Supreme, a seasoning blend for salads, was introduced by the Schilling Division.

Sales operations were established in Australia.

The era of the Orioles was led by Frank and Brooks Robinson. The Birds won the World Series, sweeping the L.A. Dodgers in four games.

In a joint venture, McCormick's Maryland Properties developed Pulaski Industrial Park in Baltimore County.

An Employee Stock Option Plan was started.

PAIN PERDU ROANOKE
(Lost Bread)

Thick, deep-fried French toast made with cornbread, crusty on the outside, moist inside.

1   10-ounce package cornbread mix
1   12-ounce can whole kernel corn
⅛ teaspoon ground Red Pepper
¼ teaspoon ground Savory
3 eggs
1 cup milk
1 tablespoon sugar
¼ teaspoon ground Nutmeg
½ teaspoon pure Vanilla Extract
Oil for frying
Confectioners' sugar
Maple syrup

Prepare cornbread batter, following package directions. Add whole kernel corn, red pepper and savory. Pour into a greased 8 x 4 x 3-inch loaf pan. Bake in 400°F. oven 30 minutes. Remove from pan. Cool. Cut in 6 thick slices. Cut each slice in half diagonally to make 12 triangular pieces. Beat eggs. Add next 4 ingredients. Mix well. Heat oil, 2 inches deep, to 350°F. Soak cornbread in egg mixture. Carefully remove each piece and lower into hot fat. Cook 4 to 5 minutes, turning once. Use a slotted spoon to lift bread out of oil. Drain on absorbent paper. Sprinkle with confectioners' sugar and serve with maple syrup.

Makes 12 pieces

Served at the 1963 World's Fair in New York.

4 eggs, beaten
1½ cups buttermilk
2 cups sifted flour
1 teaspoon baking soda
2 teaspoons baking powder
½ teaspoon salt
¼ teaspoon ground Cinnamon
⅛ teaspoon ground Nutmeg
2 tablespoons sugar
6 tablespoons melted butter
Strawberries
Whipped cream

Beat eggs. Add buttermilk. Sift dry ingredients together. Add gradually to egg mixture, beating with electric mixer. Continue beating while gradually adding melted butter. Cook in Belgian waffle iron. Use ¾ to 1 cup batter for each waffle. Cook only until lightly browned. Waffles should be soft. Serve warm with sliced sugared strawberries and whipped cream.

BATTER CAN BE MADE AHEAD   *Makes 4 cups batter, 4 to 6 waffles*

SCHILLING DVN. OF McCORMICK & CO.
DEDICATES $3 MILLION
MANUFACTURING PLANT

1968

Vietnam became the nation's longest war in June 1968.

McCormick purchased Tubed Chemicals Corporation of Easthampton, Massachusetts, a contract packer and an important producer of plastic tubes. As a wholly owned subsidiary, the name was changed to Tubed Products, Inc.

Corporate offices moved from Light Street to Executive Plaza I in Hunt Valley Business Community.

Childers Foods, Inc., of Bedford, Virginia, became a wholly owned subsidiary known as McCormick Foods, Inc. (later merged into Golden West Foods, Inc.).

McCormick products were manufactured in El Salvador and distributed throughout the entire Central American common market through a newly formed subsidiary, McCormick de Centro America, S.A.

An Australian national favorite, simple but spectacular.

4 egg whites, at room temperature
Dash salt
1 cup super-fine sugar
1 teaspoon vinegar
1 teaspoon cornstarch
1½ teaspoons pure Vanilla Extract
1 pint whipping cream
¾ cup confectioners' sugar
1 pint strawberries
3 kiwi fruit

Beat egg whites with salt. Gradually add sugar, beating until very thick. Beat in vinegar, cornstarch and ½ teaspoon of the vanilla. Grease a baking sheet and dust heavily with cornstarch. Spoon meringue onto center of baking sheet. Spread with back of spoon to make 9-inch round or oval. Bake in 275°F. oven 1 hour. Do not brown. Cool in oven with door open. Place meringue on serving plate. Whip cream with confectioners' sugar and remaining 1 teaspoon vanilla until stiff. Chill. Wash and hull strawberries. Peel and slice kiwi fruit. Save 6 whole strawberries and 6 to 8 slices kiwi for garnish. Slice remaining berries. Place sliced berries and kiwi on meringue. Spread about ⅓ of the whipped cream over fruit. Using a pastry bag with large star tip, pipe whipped cream to cover sides. Pipe large rosettes of cream around the top and bottom. Garnish with reserved fruit. Cut in wedges.

EASY
USE ANY FRESH FRUIT

Makes 8 to 10 wedges

(see photo page 84)

CHOCOLATE MERINGUE PIE

A delectable treat for dedicated chocoholics!

1¼ cups sugar
½ teaspoon salt
½ cup cornstarch
4 cups milk
4 1-ounce squares unsweetened chocolate, melted
6 eggs, separated
¼ cup butter
2 teaspoons pure Vanilla Extract
1 baked 9-inch pie shell
Meringue (recipe below)

In saucepan, combine sugar, salt and cornstarch. Gradually stir in milk and melted chocolate. Cook, stirring constantly, over medium heat until mixture comes to a boil. Remove from heat. Gradually stir small amount of the chocolate mixture into lightly beaten egg yolks. Blend egg mixture with remainder of chocolate. Return to heat, stirring constantly, until mixture boils. Remove from heat. Cool. Stir in butter and vanilla extract. Pour into prepared pie shell. Top with Meringue.

MUST DO AHEAD   *Makes one 9-inch pie*

Meringue: Combine 6 egg whites, ⅛ teaspoon ground Mace and ¼ teaspoon Cream of Tartar. Beat until foamy. Gradually beat in 1 cup sugar. Beat until stiff peaks form when beaters are lifted. Spread over pie filling, sealing to edge. Bake in preheated 375°F. oven until meringue is lightly browned. Cool out of drafts. Chill 3 to 4 hours.

1969

McCormick Foods Australia Pty. Ltd. was established as a wholly owned subsidiary in Melbourne.

A new line of packaged Mexican dinners, Taco Casserole and Tamale Pie, was marketed nationally.

Harry K. Wells was elected President. John N. Curlett was named Chairman of the Board and Chief Executive Officer. C. P. McCormick retired and became Chairman Emeritus.

Construction began by McCormick Properties on Hunt Valley Golf Course in Phoenix, Baltimore County.

A Fall classic for the children.

6 medium Red Delicious apples
6 3-inch pieces Cinnamon Stick
1 14-ounce bag vanilla caramels
½ teaspoon pure Vanilla Extract
½ teaspoon imitation Rum Extract
2 tablespoons water
⅛ teaspoon ground Cinnamon
1/16 teaspoon ground Nutmeg
1/16 teaspoon ground Allspice
Dash ground Mace

Wash apples. Dry thoroughly. Push a sturdy cinnamon stick into stem end of each apple. Set aside. Melt caramels with remaining ingredients in top of double boiler over boiling water, until smooth, stirring frequently. Keeping sauce over hot water, dip apples into hot caramel sauce and turn until apple is completely coated. Allow excess sauce to drip off apple. Place on wax paper. Refrigerate until caramel coating is firm.

MUST DO AHEAD   *Makes 6 caramel apples*

PRALINE LACE COOKIES

¼ cup butter
¼ cup light corn syrup
¼ cup light brown sugar
½ cup plus 2 tablespoons sifted flour
¼ teaspoon baking powder
⅛ teaspoon ground Nutmeg
¼ teaspoon ground Cinnamon
⅓ cup Sesame Seed, lightly toasted
54 pecan halves

Melt butter, corn syrup and brown sugar in top of double boiler over simmering water. Sift together flour, baking powder, nutmeg and cinnamon. Stir into butter mixture. Add sesame seed. Stir to blend. Drop by ½ teaspoonfuls, 3 inches apart, on greased baking sheet. Center a pecan half on each cookie. Bake in 325°F. oven 8 minutes. Cool on baking sheet about 2 minutes. Remove with thin spatula. Finish cooling on flat surface.

CAN DO AHEAD   *Makes 4½ dozen cookies*

Note: To toast sesame seed, spread in shallow baking pan and heat in 350°F. oven 10 minutes or until lightly browned.

1969

McCormick's consolidated sales reached $100 million.

Authorized shares of Common Stock increased to 900,000 shares, Non-Voting to 2.4 million, doubling each class. Stock split 2-for-1.

The ultimate youth spectacle of the decade was the Woodstock Music and Art Fair, a rock festival that drew thousands of people to a town in Sullivan County, New York.

The Company's regular line of whole spices was converted from cardboard to metal containers with plastic tops.

Turbulent Years

The anti-Vietnam War demonstrations peaked. Four students were killed at Kent State University when the National Guard fired into a group of protestors. The "classified" Pentagon papers were published. In Vietnam, a cease-fire was finally signed in 1973.

The Baltimore Colts beat the Dallas Cowboys in Super Bowl V in 1971.

President Nixon made historic trips to Russia and China. Voting rights were granted to 18-year-olds. President Nixon and Vice President Agnew were re-elected. Police arrested five men for breaking into the Democratic National Headquarters at the Watergate complex in Washington, D.C. The "Watergate Scandal" that followed would lead to the resignation of President Nixon.

An energy crisis forced cutbacks in the use of heating oil, gasoline and transportation services. Baking bread regained popularity. Recipes for cold fruit soups were in demand, especially for brunches.

Vice President Spiro Agnew was forced to resign over charges of tax evasion; Gerald Ford succeeded him. In 1974, President Nixon resigned. Gerald Ford became President.

The fad of "streaking"—running nude in public—spread across campuses and public places. Hank Aaron hit his 715th career home run, breaking Babe Ruth's record. *One Flew Over the Cuckoo's Nest* won four top Academy Awards. Star-spangled events in 1976 helped the United States celebrate its bicentennial.

Jimmy Carter, former Governor of Georgia, defeated Gerald Ford to become President in 1976. Through his influence, a peace treaty was signed by Egyptian President Anwar el-Sadat and Israeli Prime Minister Menachem Begin. American hostages were taken by Iran.

In the arts, it was a decade of one-word titles. On Broadway: *Company*, *Cabaret*, *Applause*, *Grease*, *Equus* and *Annie*. Leonard Bernstein premiered his symphonic composition *Mass*. In books, Peter Benchley's *Jaws*, Alex Haley's *Roots* and Gore Vidal's *1876* were best sellers.

"All in the Family" was the top-rated television show.

Strawberries with Brie Sauce (page 118)

16 ripe red plums
1 cup water
2 cups sugar
1 quart apple juice
6 whole Cloves
6 whole Allspice
1 4-inch piece Cinnamon Stick
1 2-inch piece Vanilla Bean
¼ teaspoon salt
2 to 3 drops Red Food Color

Cut plums in half and remove pits. In large saucepan or Dutch oven, combine water, sugar, apple juice, spices and salt. Heat to boiling. Reduce heat and simmer 10 minutes. Remove whole spices. Add plum halves. Heat to a boil. Reduce heat and simmer 10 minutes. Cool slightly. Drain liquid into glass or ceramic bowl. Put plums through a food mill or coarse strainer. Discard skins. Add plum pulp and red color to soup and mix well. Chill.

MUST DO AHEAD

Makes 2 quarts

½ cup salad oil
¼ cup vinegar
3 tablespoons sugar
¼ cup ketchup
2 teaspoons Romano Cheese Garni®
2 10-ounce bags fresh spinach
1 8-ounce can water chestnuts, drained and diced
1 8-ounce can bamboo shoots, drained
1 Bermuda onion, sliced and separated into rings
4 hard-cooked eggs, peeled and chopped
10 pieces bacon, fried crisp and crumbled

Combine first 5 ingredients in cruet or small jar. Shake well. Refrigerate at least 20 minutes to allow flavors to blend. Wash spinach. Tear in bite-size pieces. Drain well. In large salad bowl, combine spinach and remaining ingredients. Pour dressing over all and toss gently. If desired, sprinkle with additional Romano Cheese Garni.

Makes 4 quarts salad, 1 cup dressing

1970

Tubed Products acquired patent rights to produce a seamless coated plastic tube for packaging a wide variety of consumer products.

The Company launched the Adopt-A-School Program with General Henry Lee Junior High School in downtown Baltimore.

Harry K. Wells became Chief Executive Officer following John N. Curlett's retirement. Mr. Curlett remained Chairman of the Board.

The Company added Swiss Steak and Onion Burger seasoning mixes to the product line.

1971

Hunt Valley Inn, a suburban hospitality and convention center subsidiary, opened in Hunt Valley, Maryland.

A joint venture, Botanicus Pte. Ltd., was begun with the Stange Company for oleoresin production in Singapore.

Gilroy Foods established an international sales branch in a London, England, suburb.

A special salad—great for a luncheon gathering.

1 cup dry white wine
1 cup water
1 pound sea scallops
1 pound shrimp, peeled and deveined
1 pound crabmeat
1 cucumber, peeled, seeded, chopped
¼ cup mayonnaise
¼ cup dairy sour cream
½ teaspoon lemon juice
⅛ teaspoon ground Black Pepper
½ teaspoon Bon Appétit
1 teaspoon Parsley Flakes
½ teaspoon freeze-dried Chopped Chives
⅛ teaspoon Tarragon Leaves
4 avocados

Combine wine and water in medium saucepan. Heat to a boil. Reduce heat. Add scallops and shrimp. Simmer until just cooked through, about 4 minutes. Drain and allow to cool. In large bowl, combine scallops, shrimp, crabmeat and cucumber. Toss lightly. Set aside. In small bowl, combine remaining ingredients except avocados. Mix well. Pour over seafood mixture. Toss lightly until seafood mixture is evenly coated. Cover and refrigerate overnight. Cut avocados in half lengthwise. Remove seed. Spoon seafood salad over each half.

MUST DO AHEAD   *Makes 7 cups salad*

Fennel
Seed

SOLE MOUSSE
WITH SHRIMP SAUCE

1 pound filet of sole
2 cups whipping cream
4 eggs
⅔ cup milk
1 tablespoon Parsley Flakes
1½ teaspoons salt
¼ teaspoon ground Savory
⅛ teaspoon ground White Pepper
Dash ground Red Pepper
1 tablespoon butter
1 tablespoon fine dry, unseasoned, bread crumbs
¼ teaspoon Dill Weed
Shrimp Sauce (recipe below)

Cut sole in small pieces. Place about ½ cup cream in blender jar, add ¼ of the fish, and blend at medium speed until smooth. Add 1 whole egg, scrape down sides of jar with rubber spatula, and blend again until smooth. Mixture will become very thick. Turn out into a bowl, and repeat until all of the fish is blended with all of the cream. Stir milk, parsley flakes, salt, savory, white pepper and red pepper into fish mixture, blending well. Spread all the butter in a 6-cup ring mold. Combine bread crumbs and dill weed, and sprinkle over bottom and sides of mold. Spoon fish mixture into mold; level top with a spatula if necessary. Set in pan of hot water. Bake in 350°F. oven 45 minutes, until top is lightly browned and knife inserted into center comes out clean. Let stand 15 minutes and remove from mold. Serve with Shrimp Sauce.

Makes six 1-cup servings

Shrimp Sauce: Melt ¼ cup butter. Stir in 3 tablespoons flour. Add 1½ cups half-and-half, ½ teaspoon salt and ½ teaspoon Instant Onion Powder. Cook, stirring, until sauce boils and thickens. Stir in 3 tablespoons dry sherry, 1 tablespoon lemon juice and 2 teaspoons Parsley Flakes. Add 2 cups cooked and cleaned shrimp. Heat through.

Makes 3 cups sauce

1971

A new cooking concept, Roast in Bag, was introduced nationally with three Company products: Savory Oven Roasting Bag for Chicken, Pot Roast and Spareribs — later called Bag 'n Season.

The McCormick Division Hunt Valley Plant opened with 460,000 square feet of space.

SEAFOOD STEW

1972

McCormick Foods (U.K.) opened its second plant, in Ellesmere Port, England.

Shareholders voted to increase authorized shares of Common Stock to 1.6 million and Common Stock Non-Voting to 4.8 million, doubling the authorization for each class. Stock split 2-for-1.

½ cup chopped green bell pepper
1½ cups thinly sliced carrots
¼ cup olive oil
1 28-ounce can tomatoes, chopped, in liquid
1 15-ounce can tomato sauce
2 cups water
1 Bay Leaf
¼ teaspoon Seasoning Salt
¼ teaspoon coarse grind Black Pepper
1 tablespoon Instant Minced Onion
¼ teaspoon Instant Minced Garlic
1 teaspoon Parsley Flakes
½ teaspoon Basil Leaves
¾ cup rosé wine
¼ cup lemon juice
1 pound crabmeat
1 pound sea scallops
2 dozen cherrystone clams in shells
1 dozen mussels in shells
1 pound shrimp, peeled and deveined

In Dutch oven, cook green bell pepper and carrots in olive oil until tender but not brown. Add tomatoes with liquid and next 9 ingredients. Cover and heat to a boil. Reduce heat and simmer 20 minutes. Add wine and lemon juice. Continue simmering, covered, 10 minutes. Add crabmeat and scallops. Simmer 10 minutes. Wash clams and mussels in shells. Add clams, mussels and shrimp to stew. Simmer 5 to 10 minutes or until shells open. Discard any clams and mussels in shells that have not opened during cooking. Remove bay leaf.

Makes 1 gallon

MICROWAVE DIRECTIONS

Use same ingredients, changing amounts as indicated. In 3-quart microwavable casserole, combine ¼ cup (reduced from ½ cup) green bell pepper, ¾ cup (reduced from 1½ cups) carrots, and 1 tablespoon (reduced from ¼ cup) olive oil. Microcook, covered, on High 2 to 3 minutes. Add one 15-ounce can (reduced from one 28-ounce can) tomatoes chopped in liquid, one 8-ounce can (reduced from one 15-ounce can) tomato sauce, 1 cup (reduced from 2 cups) water, 1 bay leaf, ⅛ teaspoon (reduced from ¼ teaspoon) seasoning salt, ⅛ teaspoon (reduced from ¼ teaspoon) black pepper, 1½ teaspoons (reduced from 1 tablespoon) onion, ⅛ teaspoon (reduced from ¼ teaspoon) garlic, ½ teaspoon (reduced from 1 teaspoon) parsley and ¼ teaspoon (reduced from ½ teaspoon) basil. Microcook, covered, on High 5 minutes, rotating once. Add ⅓ cup (reduced from ¾ cup) wine and 2 tablespoons (reduced from ¼ cup) lemon juice. Microcook, covered, on 50% power (Medium) 5 minutes. Add ½ pound each (reduced from 1 pound each) shrimp and scallops. Microcook, covered, on 50% power (Medium) 5 minutes, stirring and rotating once. Add ½ pound (reduced from 1 pound) crabmeat. Microcook, covered, on 25% power (Low) 2 minutes. Remove from oven and let stand, covered, 5 minutes. Remove bay leaf.

Optional: Wash 1 dozen (reduced from 2 dozen) clams and ½ dozen (reduced from 1 dozen) mussels in shells. Add clams and mussels to stew. Microcook, covered, on High 2 minutes, rotating once. Microcook, covered, on 50% power (Medium) 6 to 8 minutes or until shells open, stirring and rotating once. Discard any clams and mussels in shells that have not opened during cooking.

Makes 6 cups

1972

The Company entered a joint venture with Promociones y Commisiones, S.A., of Mexico, acquiring the John Kraft Sesame Corporation of Paris, Texas. The corporation was renamed Sesame Products, Inc.

Hunt Valley Golf Club held its first Middle Atlantic Open Golf Championship Tournament. The event, co-sponsored with the P.G.A., had a $10,000 purse.

Consolidated sales — $158 million.

PINEAPPLE BRUNCH BAKE

2 whole fresh pineapples
18 to 20 slices cooked turkey breast
2 tablespoons butter
2 tablespoons flour
½ teaspoon Bon Appétit
¼ teaspoon ground White Pepper
Dash ground Allspice
Dash ground Cardamom
½ teaspoon Instant Minced Onion
1 Bay Leaf
1 cup milk
1 cup shredded Cheddar cheese

Cut tops from pineapples. Set tops aside. Peel and slice each pineapple in 9 or 10 slices. Remove core from slices. On baking pan, arrange alternating slices of turkey and pineapple in 2 groups, overlapping slices to resemble the shape of 2 pineapples. Melt butter. Stir in flour and next 5 ingredients. Cook, stirring, over low heat 2 to 3 minutes. Add bay leaf. Gradually stir in milk. Gradually add shredded cheese, stirring until cheese is melted. Remove bay leaf. Spoon sauce over both pineapples. Bake in 350°F. oven 15 minutes. If desired, broil until top of sauce is lightly browned. Using 2 large spatulas, move pineapples to serving platter. Garnish with the pineapple tops.

Makes 9 or 10 servings,
2 slices pineapple and 2 slices turkey each, with sauce

1973

McCormick acquired the entire minority stock interest of 6.4% in McCormick Properties for $850,000.

The Industrial Flavor Group was established, encompassing the activities of Botanicus, Sesame and Industrial Flavor units.

Plant expansions were completed for Schilling and Gilroy Foods in California and Club House Foods in London, Ontario, Canada.

The Company introduced Skillet Magic, a top-of-the-stove seasoning and pasta combination mix for hamburger.

ORIENTAL RICE

3 tablespoons butter
Dash ground Cloves
¼ teaspoon ground Cinnamon
¼ teaspoon ground Cardamom
⅛ teaspoon ground Allspice
⅛ teaspoon Saffron, crushed
⅛ teaspoon ground Black Pepper
2 teaspoons Garlic Salt
½ teaspoon Bon Appétit
2 tablespoons Instant Minced Onion
1 cup long grain rice
3 cups boiling water
½ cup raisins
½ cup toasted slivered almonds

Melt butter in saucepan. Add next 10 ingredients. Mix well.
Add boiling water, cover, and simmer 25 minutes. Add raisins.
Let stand, covered, 5 minutes. Sprinkle with almonds.

Makes seven ½-cup servings

1974

Golden West Foods, Inc., was founded at the Gilroy plant in California to manufacture and distribute frozen food products. The Company began offering frozen onion rings through this subsidiary.

McCormick do Brasil Produtos Alimenticios Ltda. joint venture was formed.

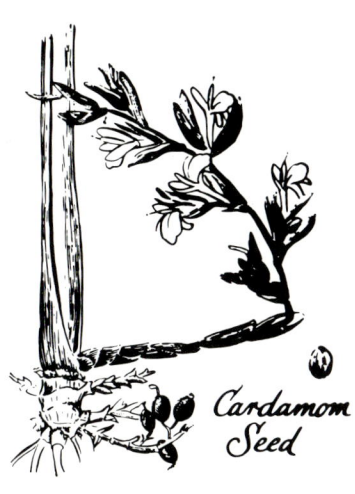

Cardamom Seed

1974

Botanicus began full production of major oleoresin spices.

An Industrial Flavor Division plant opened in Hunt Valley.

The Schilling Division introduced frozen sour dough breads topped with Cheddar, Parmesan and Romano cheeses.

A hearty casserole—wonderful served with hot bread.

2 tablespoons butter
1½ pounds pork, shoulder or loin
2 onions, thinly sliced
1 red bell pepper, cut in small strips
1 16-ounce can sauerkraut
2 cups water
2 teaspoons Beef Flavor Base
½ teaspoon Seasoning Salt
1 tablespoon Paprika
1 tablespoon Caraway Seed
1 cup dairy sour cream

Melt butter in large skillet. Cut meat in 1-inch cubes. Sauté meat with onions and bell pepper in butter. Cook 3 minutes over medium heat. Cook sauerkraut with water and beef flavor base 30 minutes. Add remaining ingredients to sauerkraut. Put sauerkraut mixture in a 2-quart casserole. Add meat mixture. Stir, if desired. Bake, covered, in 350°F. oven 30 minutes.

EASY   *Makes 6 cups*

 MICROWAVE DIRECTIONS

Use same ingredients, reducing water as indicated. In large microwavable bowl, microcook butter on 25% power (Low) 2 minutes or until melted. Cut meat in 2 x ¼-inch strips. Microcook, covered, on 50% power (Medium) 6 to 7 minutes, rotating and stirring twice. Add onions and bell pepper. Microcook, covered, on 50% power (Medium) 4 to 5 minutes. Set aside. Drain sauerkraut. In 2½-quart microwavable casserole, combine sauerkraut, ¾ cup water (reduced from 2 cups) and beef flavor base. Microcook, covered, on 50% power (Medium) 4 to 5 minutes, rotating and stirring twice. Add seasoning salt, paprika, caraway seed and sour cream. Drain meat mixture; add to casserole. Stir to blend. Microcook, covered, on 50% power (Medium) 6 to 8 minutes, rotating and stirring twice.

EASY   *Makes 6 cups*

ZESTY CHILI CON CARNE

1 pound stew beef
1 tablespoon salad oil
2½ cups water
1   6-ounce can tomato paste
2 teaspoons vinegar
3 tablespoons Chili Powder
⅛ teaspoon ground Red Pepper
1½ teaspoons Oregano Leaves
1½ teaspoons salt
⅛ teaspoon Instant Minced Garlic
¼ teaspoon ground Cumin
¼ cup Instant Chopped Onions
2 tablespoons Green Bell Pepper Flakes
2   15½-ounce cans kidney beans, drained

Cut stew beef in ½ to ¾-inch chunks. In large skillet, brown beef in hot oil on all sides. Drain excess fat. Add remaining ingredients except beans. Cover and simmer 45 minutes. Add beans. Cover and simmer 20 minutes longer.

Makes 5½ cups

MICROWAVE DIRECTIONS

Omit oil and reduce water as indicated. Cut stew beef in ¼ to ½-inch chunks. In 3-quart microwavable casserole, combine beef and 1½ cups water (reduced from 2½ cups). Microcook, covered, on 50% power (Medium) 8 to 10 minutes, rotating twice. Add remaining ingredients except beans. Microcook, covered, on 25% power (Low) 20 minutes, rotating and stirring occasionally. Add beans. Microcook, covered, on 25% power (Low) 5 minutes, stirring once. Remove from oven and let stand, covered, 5 minutes.

Makes 5 cups

1975

The two major retail units of the Company—the eastern McCormick Division and the western Schilling Division—were consolidated to form a new Grocery Products Division.

A Management Services Division was established to provide improved information services.

The Company acquired outstanding stock for $4.5 million of All Portions, Inc., manufacturers of portion-control packets of condiments, with plants in San Fernando, California; Indianapolis, Indiana; and Atlanta, Georgia.

1975

McCormick entered a joint venture with Lion Dentifrice Co., Tokyo, and made an investment with Lion and Takasago, Ltd., of Tokyo in Tokai Foods, Iwata, Japan, for the manufacture and distribution of McCormick products in Japan. McCormick-Lion Ltd. had been a McCormick licensee since 1967.

Tubed Products opened a new plant in Easthampton, Massachusetts to produce extrusion molded products.

McCormick Properties moved into its new headquarters in Hunt Valley.

2 tablespoons butter
½ teaspoon Saffron
½ teaspoon Lemon & Pepper Seasoning Salt
½ teaspoon Instant Minced Onion
1 teaspoon Chicken Flavor Base
2 tablespoons flour
1 cup water
1 tablespoon dry vermouth
1 pound fresh mushrooms, sliced
2 tablespoons butter
3 cups cubed cooked chicken

Melt butter in saucepan. Stir in next 4 ingredients. Cook 1 minute. Stir in flour. Cook, stirring, 1 minute. Gradually add water and cook, stirring constantly, until sauce is slightly thickened. Stir in vermouth. Sauté mushrooms in butter. Drain. Put mushrooms and chicken in a shallow 1-quart casserole. Pour sauce over chicken and mushrooms. Bake in 350°F. oven 15 to 20 minutes. Serve over rice, if desired.

Makes 4 cups

Note: Good use for leftover chicken or turkey.

MICROWAVE DIRECTIONS

Use same ingredients, reducing water as indicated. Place butter in large microwavable bowl. Microcook, uncovered, on 25% power (Low) 2 minutes or until melted. Stir in next 4 ingredients. Microcook, uncovered, on 25% power (Low) 1 minute. Gradually stir in flour. Microcook, uncovered, on 50% power (Medium) 1 minute. Gradually add water, reducing water to ¾ cup (from 1 cup). Microcook, uncovered, on 50% power (Medium) 4 to 5 minutes or until slightly thickened, stirring after each minute. Stir in vermouth. Set aside. Place butter in large microwavable bowl. Microcook, uncovered, on

50% power (Medium) 1 minute. Add mushrooms to bowl. Toss with melted butter. Microcook, uncovered, on 50% power (Medium) 6 to 8 minutes. Drain. Place mushrooms and chicken in a shallow 1½-quart microwavable casserole. Pour sauce over chicken and mushrooms. Toss gently. Microcook, uncovered, on 50% power (Medium) 6 to 8 minutes, rotating and stirring twice. Serve over rice, if desired.

QUICK AND EASY   *Makes 4 cups*

1976

A long-term agreement was signed with the Marriott Corporation for management of the 182-room Hunt Valley Inn and a 100-room addition by Marriott.

A parade of tall ships in the Baltimore inner harbor climaxed a meeting between President Ford and West German Chancellor Helmut Schmidt.

1976

A second Tubed Products plant was opened in Easthampton, Massachusetts, equipped primarily for the production of plastic squeeze tubes.

Consolidated sales — $304 million.

The new All Portions Plant opened in Hunt Valley.

The first corporate image advertisement for McCormick appeared in *Forbes Magazine*, in an issue spotlighting Baltimore City.

To commemorate the U.S. bicentennial, McCormick Properties sealed eight wooden boxes of documents and mementos reflecting lifestyles and work trends in a stone pillar at Hunt Valley.

A mayonnaise and salad dressing plant opened in Puerto Rico.

Construction began in South Bend, Indiana, on a new $3.5 million, 50,000-square-foot plant for the Food Service Division. It was constructed by McCormick Properties.

The Company procured raw materials from 52 countries, processed at 37 manufacturing facilities and distributed products in 84 countries.

This colorful chicken-and-rice casserole is a complete meal!

1   *2½ to 3-pound broiler/fryer chicken, cut in pieces*
1 cup finely chopped onion
1 medium green pepper, chopped
2½ teaspoons salt
1 teaspoon Oregano Leaves
½ teaspoon ground Black Pepper
½ teaspoon Instant Garlic Powder
1   *28-ounce can tomatoes, chopped, in liquid*
½ cup chopped (fully cooked) ham
¼ cup sliced green olives
3 cups water
1 teaspoon salt
¼ teaspoon Saffron, crushed
1 cup long grain rice
1   *12-ounce package frozen peas*

In Dutch oven, brown chicken on all sides. Add onion and green pepper. Sauté until tender. Add next 7 ingredients. Cover and simmer until chicken is tender. In saucepan, heat water, salt and saffron to a boil. Stir in rice. Reduce heat and simmer 20 minutes. Remove from heat and let stand 5 minutes. Cook peas, following package directions. Add rice and peas to chicken. Remove from heat. Let stand 5 to 10 minutes before serving.

Makes 6 servings, 1 piece chicken each

SAFFRON BREAD

1 cup water
⅛ teaspoon Saffron, crushed
2 teaspoons Instant Minced Onion
1   16-ounce package hot roll mix
2 tablespoons butter or margarine, softened
3 tablespoons sugar
1 egg
Egg white, beaten slightly
Caraway Seed

Heat water to a boil. Remove from heat and add saffron and onion. Cool to lukewarm (about 10 minutes). Heat oven to 200°F. for 10 minutes. Turn oven off. Combine hot roll mix with the yeast in package. Cream butter, sugar and egg until smooth; stir into roll mixture. Add the water mixture, mixing until well combined. Turn out on floured board. Knead until smooth and elastic. Shape into loaf. Place loaf in greased 9¼ x 5¼ x 2¾-inch loaf pan. Put covered pan in warmed oven to rise until nearly doubled. Bake in 375°F. oven 55 minutes. Brush crust with egg white and sprinkle with caraway seed. Bake 5 minutes longer.

EASY
CAN MAKE AHEAD

Makes one 9 x 5 x 3-inch loaf

1977

McCormick Properties acquired a 500-acre site (later named Loveton Center) for development in Baltimore County. Outside Maryland, construction was completed for the $10 million Lancaster Square (Pennsylvania) complex and the $5 million Hechinger Company of Washington, D.C.

Harry K. Wells was elected Chairman, President and Chief Executive Officer. John N. Curlett was named Chairman Emeritus.

New Company products introduced nationally included Season 'n Fry, Italian Cooking Sauce, Salt 'n Spice, Lemon 'n Herb, Top Chop and Imitation Bacon Chips.

Stock split 2-for-1.

A public offering was made of 810,000 shares of Common Stock Non-Voting through Alex Brown & Lehman Brothers, underwriters. Authorized shares increased to 4 million for Common Stock and 12 million for Common Stock Non-Voting.

The Industrial Flavor Division was renamed McCormick Flavor Division to increase recognition for the wide range of Company products.

Fun for collectors of special bread recipes.

1977

Astro Foods, Inc., of San Rafael, California, a producer of specialty frozen food products for airlines and restaurants, was purchased for $325,000 as a wholly owned subsidiary.

The sales and marketing forces of the Food Service Division and All Portions were reorganized into one unit: McCormick/All Portions Food Service Division.

Spanning the harbor, the Francis Scott Key Bridge opened and completed the Baltimore Beltway.

½ cup cornmeal
2 cups water
¼ cup butter, cut in pieces
1 ounce unsweetened chocolate
½ cup dark molasses
1½ teaspoons salt
2 tablespoons Caraway Seed
2 teaspoons instant coffee
¼ cup lukewarm water
1 ¼-ounce package active dry yeast
5½ cups flour

In saucepan, combine cornmeal and water. Cook, stirring, over medium heat until mixture comes to a boil. Simmer 1 minute. Remove from heat. Add next 6 ingredients. Stir well. Cool to lukewarm. Combine lukewarm water and yeast. Let stand 5 minutes. Stir into cornmeal mixture. Beat in 4½ cups flour, ½ cup at a time. Place dough on well-floured surface and knead in remaining flour. Continue kneading until dough is smooth and elastic, about 5 minutes. Butter inside of large bowl. Place dough in bowl. Turn dough until entire surface is lightly buttered. Cover with towel. Set in warm, draft-free place and let rise 1½ hours, or until double in size. Punch dough down. Knead 2 minutes on floured surface. Divide dough in half and shape each half into small loaf. Place each in a buttered 2¼ x 3½ x 7½-inch loaf pan. Cover with towel and let rise 40 minutes. Bake in 350°F. oven 1 hour or until loaves shrink away from sides of pan. Cool on wire racks.

Makes 2 loaves

1978

The Company's first low-calorie product, Lite Gravy, was introduced to an enthusiastic public.

Han-Dee Pak, Inc., of Atlanta, Georgia, a producer of individual condiment servings, was purchased.

Golden West Foods received its first order to produce chicken patties for a major fast-food restaurant.

Contemporary and dramatic in appearance and taste.

4 ounces Brie cheese, crust removed
½ cup whipping cream
2 teaspoons sugar
Dash ground Cardamom
¼ teaspoon pure Vanilla Extract
Dash Orange Extract
Whole fresh strawberries, chilled

Trim crust from Brie. Allow cheese to soften at room temperature. Cut in small pieces. Put whipping cream, sugar and cardamom in top of double boiler over simmering water. Heat until sugar dissolves. Add Brie. Stir occasionally while Brie melts. Remove from heat when smooth and creamy. Add extracts. Stir to mix well. Spoon sauce over whole, chilled strawberries.

QUICK—IF CHEESE IS SOFTENED   *Makes ¾ cup*

(see photo page 100)

Note: Must be prepared just before serving.

Coriander Seed

CARDAMOM APPLE PIE

A wonderful flavor added to the all-time American favorite!

Pastry for two-crust pie shell, 9-inch
7 cups peeled, cored and sliced tart apples
½ cup brown sugar
½ teaspoon ground Cardamom
¼ teaspoon ground Cinnamon
⅛ teaspoon salt
¾ teaspoon pure Vanilla Extract
2 tablespoons butter

Line a 9-inch pie plate with ½ of the pastry. Place apples in a large bowl. Combine next 4 ingredients. Toss together with apples. Place in pastry-lined pie pan. Sprinkle with vanilla extract. Dot with butter. Position top pastry over apples. Seal and flute edges. Make four slits in top pastry. Bake in 400°F. oven 10 minutes. Reduce heat to 350°F. and continue baking 40 to 45 minutes, or until crust is lightly browned.

Makes one 9-inch pie

1979

McCormick Properties broke ground in Columbia, Maryland, for the first commercial property project in the Baltimore-Washington corridor.

Gilroy Foods dedicated a solar energy project to be used to generate electricity for the dehydration of onions and garlic.

Harry K. Wells was elected Chairman of the Board and Chief Executive Officer, and Hillsman V. Wilson, President and Chief Operating Officer.

A revised edition of *Spices of the World Cookbook by McCormick* was published by McGraw-Hill.

A $3.5 million plant in Bedford, Virginia, opened for production of frozen extruded onion rings by Golden West Foods.

The New Premium Imitation Vanilla Extract was marketed, culminating five years of research.

Age of the Yuppies

The decade opened with a bang! Mount St. Helens erupted in Washington State, spewing ash 12 miles into the air over cities and farms in four states and turning 150 miles into a deathscape.

Less than an hour after Ronald Reagan was inaugurated 40th U.S. President, 52 hostages were released by Iran. Two months later, the President was wounded by a would-be assassin.

It was the "age of the commodity"—a resurgence of conspicuous consumption. Reebok® tennis shoes, Cabbage Patch Kids®, BMWs, microwave ovens and rentals of videotapes stole consumers' hearts. The Coca-Cola Company tried to change its formula for "Coca-Cola," but the public demanded the return of "The Real Thing."

In 1984, President Reagan, aged 73 and the oldest President in U.S. history—was reelected by a landslide vote, carrying 49 of 50 states.

Remains of the ill-fated *Titanic* were found 12,000 feet below sea level off the coast of Newfoundland.

In 1985, the space shuttle *Challenger* completed a flight of 2.9 million miles. Carrying animals and seven astronauts, it brought back a treasure of space research data. But this success was followed in 1986 by the *Challenger*'s tragic crash on takeoff, which caused a halt in the U.S. space program.

Drug traffic, terrorism, TV evangelists, hostages, insider trading, the AIDS epidemic and the debate over aid to Contra rebels in Nicaragua held the public spotlight.

Sandra Day O'Connor became the first woman named to the U.S. Supreme Court. Geraldine Ferraro was the first woman nominated by a major party as a candidate for Vice President, and Sally Ride became the first American woman astronaut.

The marriage of Great Britain's Charles, Prince of Wales, to Lady Diana Spencer was telecast to millions around the world.

On Black Monday, October 19, 1987, the Dow Jones lost 508 points, 22 percent of its value—the worst day in stock market history. Some called it the end of the "yuppie" years.

Many Americans stopped smoking and exercised more. Lifestyles centered on keeping fit and on eating less salt and sugar. White and "lite" foods and drinks were popular. White wine, gin, "lite" beer, vodka, chicken, fish and pasta dominated party menus. Szechuan, sushi and ethnic food trends were balanced with a resurgence of regional American dishes like Cajun and Creole.

Top Broadway shows included *Cats*, *Les Miserables*, *Phantom of the Opera*, *La Cage Aux Folles*, *The Real Thing* and *Fences*.

"Miami Vice" and the "Bill Cosby Show" replaced "Dallas" and "Dynasty" as top-rated television shows.

Pasta Primavera (page 128)

TORTILLA SOUP

This is a meal in one bowl, with a marvelous, rich blend of spice flavors.

1 cup tomato juice
½ cup coarsely chopped celery
½ cup thinly sliced carrots
7 cups hot water
2 tablespoons Beef Flavor Base
2 whole Black Peppercorns
1 Bay Leaf
1 tablespoon Instant Minced Onion
¼ teaspoon Instant Garlic Powder
1 4-ounce can mild green chillies,
drained and cut in strips
2 whole Hot Chillies
Meatballs (recipe opposite)
Tortilla chips
Monterey Jack cheese, shredded

Place first 11 ingredients in large saucepan. Heat to a boil. Reduce heat and simmer 25 minutes. Remove black peppercorns, bay leaf and hot chillies. To serve soup, place a few meatballs in soup plate. Ladle broth over meatballs. Add a few tortilla chips and sprinkle with shredded cheese.

Makes 7 cups broth

MICROWAVE DIRECTIONS

Use same ingredients, reducing water as indicated. Place first 3 ingredients in large microwavable bowl. Microcook, uncovered, on High 5 minutes. Add 5 cups water (reduced from 7 cups) and next 7 ingredients. Microcook, uncovered, on High 20 minutes, rotating and stirring 4 times. Remove black peppercorns, bay leaf and hot chillies. To serve soup, place a few meatballs in soup plate. Ladle broth over meatballs. Add a few tortilla chips and sprinkle with shredded cheese.

Makes 6 cups broth

Meatballs: In large bowl, mix 1 tablespoon Instant Minced Onion, ¼ cup fine dry, unseasoned, bread crumbs, ¼ cup milk and 1 beaten egg. Add ½ pound ground beef, ½ pound ground pork, ½ cup chopped blanched almonds, ⅛ teaspoon ground Black Pepper, ⅛ teaspoon ground Oregano, ⅛ teaspoon ground Cumin, 1 teaspoon Chervil Leaves, ½ teaspoon Shredded Green Onion and ¾ teaspoon Bon Appétit. Mix well. Shape in 1¼-inch meatballs. Heat 1 tablespoon peanut oil in large skillet. Cook meatballs 5 minutes, turning to brown on all sides. Add small amount of oil if necessary.

Makes 20 to 22 meatballs

MICROWAVE DIRECTIONS

Prepare meatballs as noted above. Omit peanut oil. Arrange meatballs in a microwavable 10-inch pie plate. Microcook, covered, on 50% power (Medium) 6 to 8 minutes, turning and rearranging meatballs once. Let stand 2 minutes. Drain excess liquid.

Makes 20 to 22 meatballs

1981

Construction began in Inglewood Business Community, a 235-acre industrial park in Prince Georges County, Maryland. A 53-acre tract at Shawan Business Center, Baltimore County, was dedicated.

Setco, Inc., a producer of stock and custom-designed plastic bottles in Culver City, California, was purchased as a subsidiary for about $7 million.

Stange Company of Chicago was purchased as a subsidiary for $24 million. Stange was known worldwide for its excellence in creating specialty flavorings, colorings and breadings and batters for the industrial and institutional food processing industries.

Setco began serving both coasts by opening a new manufacturing, warehousing and distribution facility in Monroe Township, New Jersey.

McCormick Properties agreed to sell five buildings to their lessee, Westinghouse Electric, for $17 million over four years.

The Schilling unit of McCormick celebrated its 100th anniversary.

1982

Baltimore's Joseph Meyerhoff Symphony Hall opened with a nationally televised concert.

Stange and the McCormick Flavor Division merged, forming the McCormick-Stange Flavor Division, based in Hunt Valley.

Golden West Foods moved its headquarters from Salinas, California, to Bedford, Virginia.

McCormick Properties was selected to develop, market and manage a 22-acre Foreign Trade Zone in Baltimore.

McCormick announced the filing and simultaneous settlement of an action brought in Federal District Court for the District of Columbia by the Securities and Exchange Commission alleging violations by the Company of the periodic reporting and internal accounting control provisions of the Securities Exchange Act of 1934.

McCormick Construction Company, Inc., was formed as a design/build subsidiary of McCormick Properties.

A majority interest (70%) in Produtos Alimenticios Linguanotto, Ltda., a Brazilian spice packer based in São Paulo, was purchased.

The 50th anniversary of Multiple Management was observed.

The Board of Directors voted to increase the authorized shares of the Company's Common Stock from 4 million to 10 million and Common Stock Non-Voting from 12 million to 30 million shares.

The first two individuals outside the Company to be elected to the Board of Directors were Erskine N. White, Jr., and James S. Cook.

A good salad for winter buffets.

Arrange 2 cups each cooked vegetables: green beans, carrots, cauliflower and beets in large bowl. Serve with Tarragon Salad Dressing (recipe below) or pour dressing over vegetables and marinate overnight.

Tarragon Salad Dressing: In medium bowl, beat 4 egg yolks until smooth. Gradually beat in ½ cup vegetable oil. Beat well. Add ¼ cup vinegar and ¼ teaspoon each Instant Garlic Powder, Seasoning Salt, cracked Black Pepper and Tarragon Leaves. Blend. Serve over vegetable salad.

EASY
CAN DO AHEAD

Makes 1 cup dressing

"SHOW STOPPER" SOUP

The flavors of Oysters Rockefeller, in a creamy soup.

1 10-ounce package frozen chopped spinach
3½ cups milk
½ cup drained oysters
¼ cup butter
¼ cup flour
¼ teaspoon ground Nutmeg
½ teaspoon ground White Pepper
2 teaspoons Instant Minced Onion
1 teaspoon Chicken Flavor Base
¾ teaspoon Bon Appétit
1 cup whipping cream
Whipping cream for garnish
Crushed Red Pepper

Thaw spinach; drain excess liquid. Pour 1½ cups of the milk into blender jar. Gradually add spinach, blending until smooth after each addition. Pour into a bowl. Purée oysters in blender. Add to spinach mixture. Set aside. Melt butter in large saucepan. Stir in next 6 ingredients. Cook over medium heat until bubbly. Stir in spinach mixture. Add remaining 2 cups milk and 1 cup whipping cream. Cook, stirring constantly, over medium heat until mixture begins to boil. Reduce heat and simmer 2 minutes. Garnish with dollops of unsweetened whipped cream topped with crushed red pepper.

Makes six 1-cup servings

1983

The Baltimore Orioles won the Series, beating the Philadelphia Phillies in five games.

Club House Foods observed its 100th anniversary.

McCormick Properties sold the Executive Plaza Office Center ($46 million) and interest in the Hunt Valley Inn ($28 million) to Prudential Insurance Company of America. The Hunt Valley Golf Club was sold to American Golf Corporation. Groundbreaking was held for a new Westinghouse facility. Inglewood Centre off the Washington, D.C., beltway opened.

McCormick Properties and Nottingham Properties, Inc., announced plans for the White Marsh (Maryland) High-Tech Center.

A new R&D Technical Center opened in Hunt Valley.

1984

McCormick International Investments Limited, a wholly owned subsidiary, acquired Paterson Jenks, a publicly held United Kingdom corporation, for approximately $54 million (U.S.). This marked the largest acquisition in McCormick history.

McCormick Properties entered the Sunbelt with the purchase of 23.5 acres for industrial park development in St. Petersburg, Florida.

A new Spice Mill Division was formed and a 150,000-square-foot spice mill and cleaning plant in Hunt Valley was opened. This consolidated all East Coast spice processing.

McCormick was included in the book *The 100 Best Companies to Work For in America.*

A light sauce, touched with curry, for an impromptu luncheon or quick supper.

2 tablespoons butter
2 tablespoons flour
½ teaspoon Onion Salt
½ teaspoon Bon Appétit
½ teaspoon Dill Weed
¼ teaspoon ground White Pepper
¼ teaspoon Marjoram Leaves
Dash ground Red Pepper
1 teaspoon freeze-dried Chopped Chives
2 teaspoons Madras Curry Powder
2 cups milk
1 15½-ounce can red salmon, drained
Egg noodles

In saucepan, melt butter. Stir in flour and next 8 ingredients. Cook over low heat 1 minute. Gradually stir in milk. Heat to boiling. Remove skin and bones from salmon. Break up large pieces. Add salmon to sauce. Keep hot. Serve sauce over cooked egg noodles.

QUICK AND EASY   *Makes 3½ cups sauce*

MICROWAVE DIRECTIONS

Use same ingredients, reducing milk as indicated. Place butter in large microwavable bowl. Microcook, uncovered, on 25% power (Low) 1½ minutes or until melted. Gradually blend in flour and next 8 ingredients. Microcook, uncovered, on 25% power (Low) 2 minutes, stirring twice. Gradually stir in 1½ cups (reduced from 2 cups) milk. Microcook, uncovered, on 50% power (Medium) 5 to 7 minutes, stirring after each minute. Remove skin and bones from salmon. Break up large pieces. Add salmon to sauce. Microcook, uncovered, on 25% power (Low) 4 to 6 minutes, rotating and gently stirring twice. Serve over cooked egg noodles.

QUICK AND EASY   *Makes 2⅔ cups sauce*

1984

Arrangements totaling approximately $2.5 million were completed with N.P.I., a plant biotechnology company in Salt Lake City, Utah, which produces, markets and distributes plant and seed materials.

Announcement was made of the intended repurchase of up to 500,000 shares of Company stock for employee stock plans.

Expansion of Food Service plants in South Bend, Indiana; Doraville, Georgia; and Hunt Valley were completed.

Reduced Sodium Garlic and Onion Salt, Lemon and Pepper Seasoning, Season-All and Fried Chicken Seasoning were added to the product line.

PASTA PRIMAVERA

1985

Spice Classics, an economy line of spices, was introduced for distribution by non-grocery outlets.

A new Gourmet line of spices, featuring enhanced product quality and upscaled packaging, was introduced. A $1 million advertising campaign was geared toward educating the consumer about spices and how to use them. The campaign slogan was "McCormick/Schilling Gourmet. Quite simply, the best spices on earth."

The McCormick-Stange Flavor Division reached an agreement to sell its Keratene Hydrolyzed Vegetable Protein (HVP) operation in Winsted, Connecticut, to Champlain Industries, Limited of Toronto, Canada.

New-wave Italian dish with a rich, creamy sauce.

6 ounces fettucini (yields 3 cups cooked)
¼ cup butter
1 tablespoon flour
½ teaspoon Instant Garlic Powder
¼ teaspoon Instant Onion Powder
¼ teaspoon Parsley Flakes
Dash ground Nutmeg
⅛ teaspoon ground White Pepper
¼ teaspoon Bon Appétit
¾ cup whipping cream
½ cup shredded Havarti cheese
½ cup carrots, cut in sticks (¼ x ¼ x 1 inch)
1 cup broccoli florets
1 cup Italian green beans, cut in 1-inch pieces
½ cup Italian plum tomatoes, peeled and coarsely chopped

Cook fettucini while preparing sauce. Melt butter in a 2-quart saucepan. Gradually stir in flour and seasonings. Cook 1 minute, stirring with wire whisk. Gradually add cream and shredded cheese. Stir until cheese melts. Drain fettucini and put in large warmed bowl. Add vegetables and sauce. Toss and serve immediately.

Makes 4½ cups

(see photo page 120)

A hot cucumber salad—an excellent use for winter cucumbers.

4 slices bacon
2 cucumbers
1 medium red pepper
1 small yellow onion
⅛ teaspoon ground White Pepper
¼ teaspoon Celery Seed
¼ teaspoon Seasoning Salt
¼ teaspoon Parsley Flakes
¼ teaspoon sugar
3 tablespoons water
2 tablespoons red wine vinegar
½ teaspoon cornstarch

Fry bacon. Drain. Reserve 2 tablespoons bacon fat. Set aside. Peel, quarter, and seed cucumbers. Cut in julienne strips. Seed red pepper. Cut in thin bite-size strips. Peel onion and cut in ⅛-inch slices. Separate onion into rings. Heat bacon fat in skillet over medium-high heat. Add cucumbers, red peppers and onion. Stir-fry 3 minutes. Remove vegetables from skillet. Combine remaining 8 ingredients. Mix well. Add to skillet, stirring constantly, until mixture thickens. Add vegetables and heat through. Arrange cucumbers, peppers and onion on 4 salad plates. Garnish each serving with crumbled bacon.

Makes 3 cups, enough for 4 individual salads

1985

$25 million, which represented 15% of the market value of the equity of McCormick Properties, was transferred to the parent company McCormick to facilitate a buy-back of up to 10% of its common stock.

McCormick Properties and Creaney & Smith formed a joint venture to purchase AT&T's Broening Highway facilities.

The C-Day Program was honored with a Presidential Citation during a White House ceremony.

Gilroy Foods purchased the assets of Geothermal Food Processors, Inc., of Brady's Hot Springs, Nevada. The firm uses geothermal energy as its heat source to dehydrate onions.

McCormick do Brasil purchased Industria E Comercio Jimmi Ltda. of São Paulo, Brazil, a producer of pourable sauces, mustard, pickles and other condiments.

Setco purchased the assets of Poly-Vue Plastics Corporation of Petaluma, California.

1986

A new specialty product line, Classic American Foods, was introduced. The line included wine mustards, shake-on seasoning blends, creole mustard, sauces and a butter pecan dessert topping. The Company also introduced Pasta Prima, a line of high-quality authentic pasta sauce blends.

Setco moved into a new plant in Anaheim, California, becoming the largest injection blow-molding operation in the world.

Ground was broken for a $92 million gas-fired cogeneration project for Gilroy Foods. Cogeneration is the process by which two different types of energy—steam and electricity—are produced from the same source, gas.

McCormick Construction Company acquired the North Carolina construction firm Myers & Chapman, Inc.

15 broiler/fryer chicken wings
1 cup flour
¼ cup Sesame Seed
½ teaspoon ground White Pepper
½ teaspoon Poultry Seasoning
2 teaspoons Seasoning Salt
Dash ground Nutmeg
2 eggs
2 tablespoons water
Oil for frying
Sweet and Sour Dunk (recipe below)

Cut each chicken wing in 3 pieces, cutting at joints. Discard tips. Combine next 6 ingredients. Beat together eggs and water. Dip chicken pieces in egg mixture, then roll in flour mixture. Fry in 375°F. oil until golden brown. Drain on absorbent paper. Serve hot with Sweet and Sour Dunk.

Makes 30 pieces

Sweet and Sour Dunk: Combine ¾ cup sugar, 2 tablespoons cornstarch, 1½ teaspoons Paprika and ¼ teaspoon salt. Stir until mixture is well blended. Slowly stir in ½ cup water and ⅓ cup vinegar. Add 2 teaspoons Green Bell Pepper Flakes. Cook over medium heat, stirring constantly, until mixture comes to a boil. Simmer 1 minute.

Makes 1 cup sauce

A refreshing change and an excellent buffet dish.

2 boneless half turkey breasts
1 10-ounce package pitted dates
1 16-ounce package dried apricot halves
1 cup walnut pieces
2 cups water
½ teaspoon ground Cinnamon
¼ teaspoon ground Black Pepper
¼ teaspoon ground Ginger
¼ teaspoon ground Nutmeg
¼ teaspoon ground Cloves

Cut 3 parallel, lengthwise, 1-inch deep slits in each turkey breast half. Place turkey breast halves flat in a buttered roasting pan. Cut dates in thirds. Cut apricot halves in fourths. Combine dates, apricots and remaining ingredients in saucepan. Heat, stirring constantly. Simmer 2 minutes, stirring. Cool slightly. Fill slits in turkey with fruit mixture. Cook in 325°F. oven 2 hours. Cut each breast half in 6 slices.

EASY   *Makes 12 generous servings*

1986

The McCormick Collection, a specialty shop on the first floor of the Light Street building, opened. A catalog, American Accents, offered specialty items to the general public.

Tio Sancho Mexican food production was relocated to Prince Frederick, Maryland.

Tea manufacturing operations ceased in Hunt Valley, shifting to a contract packer in Marietta, Georgia.

McCormick purchased a half interest in Festin Foods Corp. of Carlsbad, California, an importer of Mexican foods owned by the Herdez Group, a leading Mexican food processor.

Following the success of the revamped Gourmet line, a restyled retail line of basic spices, seasonings and flavoring products packaged in plastic was introduced.

The Armanino Farms business of G. Armanino & Son, Inc., of San Francisco, California, the world's largest grower and processor of chives, was acquired.

McCormick Properties added two outside directors to its Board of Directors.

Ginger

1987

In February, Charles P. McCormick, Jr., was elected President and Chief Executive Officer. Bailey A. Thomas was elected Executive Vice President and Chief Operating Officer.

The Unsung Heroes Banquet for the first time included female honorees for basketball. A total of 64 schools and 99 students participated.

Brennan's of New Orleans, a line of Cajun/Creole foods, was promoted by the Company. The 19-item product line included spice blends, coatings and mixes, condiments, dessert toppings and coffees.

McCormick Properties celebrated its 25th anniversary by opening CenterPointe, a 128,000-square-foot office building in Hunt Valley.

The Grocery Products Division's name officially changed to the McCormick/Schilling Division.

Three California acquisitions totaling $35 million in revenues were completed—Gentry Foods in Gilroy, producer of dehydrated onions and garlic; Parsley Patch in Windsor, salt-free and sugar-free spice blends; and The Herb Farm in Encinitas, largest grower and marketer of fresh herbs.

$1 billion in sales achieved.

A spectacular dessert for special dinner parties.

2 envelopes unflavored gelatine
1½ cups canned pineapple juice, chilled
8 eggs, separated
½ teaspoon salt
1 cup sugar
⅛ teaspoon ground Mace
⅛ teaspoon ground Cardamom
½ teaspoon imitation Rum Extract
1 cup whipping cream
2 tablespoons confectioners' sugar
¼ cup dark rum
1 cup cream of coconut
Sweetened whipped cream

Soften gelatine in ½ cup of the cold pineapple juice. In top of double boiler, combine egg yolks, salt, ¼ cup of the sugar, mace, cardamom and the remaining 1 cup pineapple juice. Cook over boiling water, stirring constantly, until slightly thickened. Add gelatine mixture and rum extract. Stir until gelatine is dissolved. Pour into a large bowl. Cool. To prepare 6-cup soufflé dish, fold a 30-inch strip of foil in half lengthwise. Tie foil with string around outside of dish to make a collar standing about 5 inches above rim. Beat egg whites until foamy. Gradually add the remaining ¾ cup sugar. Beat until stiff peaks form when beaters are lifted. Whip cream with confectioners' sugar. Add rum and cream of coconut to gelatine mixture. Stir well. Gently fold in egg whites and whipped cream. Pour into prepared soufflé dish. Refrigerate at least 3 hours. Cut string and carefully remove foil collar. Garnish soufflé with sweetened whipped cream.

MUST DO AHEAD

Makes sixteen ½-cup servings

1988

Stange Canada of Mississauga, Ontario, Canada, acquired Flavour Ingredients Limited (also known as Food Ingredients), also of Mississauga.

Charles P. McCormick, Jr., was elected Chairman of the Board and Chief Executive Officer. Bailey A. Thomas was elected President and Chief Operating Officer.

The Company announced that all of its real estate properties, including property holdings in downtown Baltimore, were offered for sale as one package.

Stock split 2-for-1 in both classes of common stock. A repurchase program of up to 5% of outstanding shares was announced.

Rich, traditional truffles can now be concocted on the spur of the moment.

24 ounces semi-sweet chocolate chips
2 tablespoons butter
2 tablespoons dairy sour cream
½ teaspoon imitation Brandy Extract
½ teaspoon imitation Rum Extract
½ teaspoon pure Vanilla Extract
Unsweetened cocoa powder
Flaked coconut
Finely chopped pecans

Put chocolate, butter and sour cream in a 3-quart microwavable casserole. Microcook, covered, on High 2 minutes. Stir thoroughly. Microcook, covered, on High 1 minute longer. Stir. Divide mixture into three portions. Add one extract to each portion and mix well. Shape into 1-inch balls and roll in cocoa, coconut or chopped pecans. Store in airtight container.

QUICK AND EASY   *Makes 50 truffles*

WHOLE WHEAT PUMPKIN MUFFINS

Rich, moist and flavorful, this recipe will become a favorite.

1½ cups sugar
1 16-ounce can pumpkin (2 cups)
3 eggs
½ cup salad oil
1 cup water
1½ cups sifted flour
1½ cups sifted whole wheat flour
1½ teaspoons baking powder
1 teaspoon baking soda
1 teaspoon salt
¾ teaspoon ground Cinnamon
¼ teaspoon ground Cloves
1¼ teaspoons ground Nutmeg
1½ cups raisins
1 cup coarsely chopped walnuts

Preheat oven to 400°F. Combine sugar, pumpkin, eggs, oil and water. Beat at low speed 1 minute. Sift together both flours and next 6 ingredients. Add to pumpkin mixture. Stir just until dry ingredients are moistened. Stir in raisins and nuts. Spoon into lightly greased muffin pans (2½-inch diameter). Bake in preheated 400°F. oven 20 to 22 minutes.

EASY   *Makes 2½ dozen muffins*

1989

McCormick commemorates its centennial milestone with a year of celebration for its customers, employees, shareholders and suppliers.

McCORMICK & COMPANY, INC.

1. *The Abbott Almanac—100 Years of Commitment to Quality Health Care,* The Benjamin Co., Inc., Elmsford, NY, 1988.

2. *American Cooking,* edited by Dale Brown, Time-Life Books, New York, NY, 1968.

3. *Chronicle of the 20th Century,* Chronicle Publications, Mt. Kisco, NY, 1987.

4. "Etiquette in the 80's," *SUN Magazine, Baltimore Sun,* Baltimore, MD, Jan. 10, 1988.

5. *First Ladies Cookbook,* Parent's Magazine Press, New York, NY, 1976.

6. *Front Page,* Gallery Books, W.H. Smith Publishers, Inc., New York, NY, 1985.

7. *Hammond Almanac—1983,* 14th Edition, edited by Martin A. Bacheller, New York Times Co., New York, NY, 1983.

8. "Man à la Mode," *Ligature,* Volume V, No. 1, World Typeface Center, Inc., New York, NY, 1987.

9. *Quintessence,* by Betty Cornfield and Owen Edwards, Crown Publishers, Inc., New York, NY, 1983.

10. *Restaurant and Institution Magazine,* Cahners Publishing Co., Inc., Nov. 1987.

11. "Selected Recipes That Keep the Family Happy," McCormick & Company, Baltimore, MD, 1927.

12. "Ten Most Famous Ten-Year-Olds in History," advertisement, *USA Today,* September 15, 1987.

13. "The 30's and the 40's," *Woman's Day Magazine,* CBS Magazines, New York, NY, October 1987.

14. "Things Aren't Really Happening," *Baltimore Sun,* Baltimore, MD, Nov. 3, 1987.

15. "This is McCormick," McCormick & Company, Inc., Hunt Valley, MD, 1984.

16. *Timetables of History,* edited by Bernard Grun, Simon and Schuster, New York, NY, 1975.

17. *World Almanac—1986,* Newspaper Enterprise Assn., Inc., New York, NY, 1986.

18. *World Book Encyclopedia,* Vol. 7, 18, 20, Field Enterprises Educational Corporation, Chicago, IL, 1963.